DEDICATION

This book is dedicated to God Almighty to my Saviour Jesus Christ, and to the Holy Spirit who inspired me to write this book.

Acknowledgements

To my mother a big thank you for your support and prayers for me and for being a cheer leader in my life

To my late dad Reuben Salimu for emphasising humility in my life

To my mentor, Dr Mike Murdock for teaching me the three most important things in my life, the Holy Spirit, the Seed and the Assignment

To my children Chilande, Musonda, Lawrence, Musama and Lubuto for loving me and for your support

To my son in law Francesco Marino for being in my life and for coming through for me when I needed much help

To my daughters in law Charlene and Queen for being in my life

To Pastor Peggy Mwape of Christian Bible Church for interceding for me since day one when I gave my life to the Lord to date and for being a sister to me

To my cousin Frederick Ross for being more than a brother to me and your support

To my cousin Nana Simanwe for being more than a sister to me and a cheer leader assuring me all is well

To my brother in law Dr Wilfred Simanwe for all you have done and for being a blessing

To my grandchildren Sydney, Lorenza, Chichi, Mwimba, Jayden,Miracle and Lenewa, you make my days

To my sisters Judith and Mwimba for the part you have played in my life

To Pastor Sam Appiah Addu of Follow-Up Department at KICC for teaching me the importance of midnight prayers

To the Prayer Team of Follow-Up department at KICC, brother Emmanuel Brown, brother Frank Kuofie, Sister Mamere Kef-Kamara, Sister Folashade

1

Onuluwo, Sister Olufemi Abe, Sister Jeffline Nyame, Sister Rita and Sister Kemi for your commitment and dedication to prayer, an awesome team.

Special Thanks to my son in law Steve Heppell for the graphics

Special thanks to my daughter Musama for pushing me to complete the manuscript and for editing

Scripture

"Now this is the confidence we have in Him, that if we ask anything according to His will, he hears us. And if we know that He hears us whatever we ask, we know that we have the petitions that we have asked of Him" 1 John 5:14-15

Florence Salimu Mponda gave her life to the Lord over 29 years ago. She loves to pray and loves to hear and obey the voice of the Holy Spirit. She is an intercessor, author, and teacher. She worked as a Personal Secretary to the Assistant Director Personnel, Administration and Operations at Bank of Zambia for 21 years where she pioneered the BOZ Lunch Hour Christian Fellowship. She was a member of the Zambia Intercessory Network and was a Vice Chairperson of the Intercession Team at the Assemblies of God Church in Zambia where she pioneered the Visitation and Follow up Team. She was a member of the Pan African Women Alliance (PACWA). She is a Registered Nurse by profession, a widow and has five children and seven grand children

This is the confidence that we have in Him, that if we ask anything according to His will, He hears us. And if we know that He hears us, whatever we ask, we know that we have the petitions that we have asked of Him. 1 John 5:14-15

Testimonies

As a mother I find Florence as a spring of water in my life. She is like a tree planted in water, which bears leaves that do not dry, always doing and displaying goodness and never has done anything wrong to me. I ask God to add more years to her life. **Irene Ross**

Florence is a name that immediately conjures an image of beauty and compassion. I have known Florence for a few years now and have always found her to be a very spiritual and caring person. Always thinking of the needs of others, she is incredibly selfless, forever striving through both her prayers and deep devotion to God as well as through her own skills as a nurse to help those around her. **Alicia**

Thank you for your wonderful support through prayers. Your special gift enabled me to let go of past sad memories and sorrows. My life is now enriched with God's blessings and joy. It is like a miracle.

Your spiritual strength and gift gives love and hope to others. May you continue with your mission and may the Lord bless you in your entire journey. Words cannot express my gratitude to you and I am blessed you came into my life. **Maria**

To Florence, an angel without wings

I was going through a very difficult time in my life. I had separated from my partner of many years and with a small child I was struggling financially. I turned to Florence and she provided me with the most powerful prayers and before I knew it, my prayers were answered. I found a new home, a job and money to provide for my son. **Marcia**

WHY I WROTE THIS BOOK

To mark my sixtieth birthday the Lord told me to write a book and thus this book "My Walk With God" was birthed. It is my prayer that what has been written in this book will encourage someone out there to know that there is a true God who is able to heal, deliver and set free. It took me a while for me to find healing, deliverance and freedom from demonic oppression because I first tried in my own power to find a solution but I was looking in the wrong direction and thus yielded no result. After many years of suffering with oppression and trying everything I knew with no help, I then turned to God who had the answers to all my problems.

I would not like anyone else to go through sickness, oppression and any form of bondage and struggle on their own like I did which took me such a long time to discover the mighty power of the Lord Jesus Christ of Nazareth. I had been through so much torment and oppression that I did not know where the solution would come from. Everyday I did not know how that day would end. As much as I loved my children and do love them and cared for them to the best of my ability I could not provide the care they deserved at that time as I depended on my house help, my mother, my young sister and my late husband to care for them as I was always focussed on looking for a solution for my problem which led to my being out of my home seeking solutions most of the time. Thankfully, as I called on God, He had mercy on me and the dramatic change came as He came into my life.

Having been lost without hope and later receiving salvation through Jesus Christ, it was such a miraculous turn around when God started manifesting His power and His presence in my life to the extent that I have had supernatural encounters such as the Lord Jesus Himself appearing to me in my dream and I have had numerous angelic encounters as explained in detail in the chapters ahead. I have become more sensitive to the voice of the Holy Spirit, His guidance and direction. God has revealed things to me through visions and dreams and in other various ways. Having had lots of supernatural encounters does not mean I have arrived as I am still seeking, learning, growing and yearning for more of Him and because of that I am teachable.

The Christian walk is a journey which enables us grow from one stage to another. When I started having angelic encounters I did not have the unction from the Holy Spirit then to say much about these experiences until now. When the Lord Jesus Christ appeared to me in the dream it was so real I can clearly remember like it was yesterday and the angelic visitations have occurred in ways I had never dreamed of as will be explained later. However, as Dr Mike Murdock says in one of his books, if your spiritual encounter does not bring you closer to God and bond you with the Holy Spirit, then it has merely been an experience.

I have written this book to encourage everyone that God saves, heals and delivers and will use any vessel that is yielded to his Spirit and His will. God is not a respecter of persons. What he has done for me and through me, He can do to anyone willing to walk and abide in the Lord.

THE BEGINNING OF MY WALK WITH GOD

I was born from a family that went to church which meant that I knew about going to church to pray but, my conviction was not that strong until when I passed to go to Year eight.

I was privileged to go to a Catholic boarding school, which was run by Dominican nuns. I call it a privilege because every parent wished their girl child would go to such schools due to its high level of standards of education and moral character building based on Christian principles. Once at Ibenga Girls School we were taught the Christian way of life and part of our curriculum was Religious Education. We were also given rotas to attend early morning mass for prayers before going to class. This habit became part of me and I found myself more and more interested in prayer and things of God. I have learnt in life that every habit that is repeated increases in life and every habit which increases in one's life finally takes control of your life finally takes control of your life.

Fortunately for me it was a good habit, which I embraced. My childhood friend Catherine was one of the people that were chosen to lead worship songs in church, therefore we found ourselves in church most of the time like Benediction, which was evening service during the week and at weekends too. I used to admire the people who would receive Holy Communion but in the Catholic Church, you could only receive Holy Communion after water baptism. I therefore registered for baptism classes and was baptized. I was so glad as I put on the white baptismal dress and white veil that signified purity. I later received Confirmation that signalled one's firm Christian commitment in the

Catholic Church. I felt such a joy when I finally was able to receive Holy Communion which I couldn't receive before baptism. By God's grace I grew in my Christian walk and was committed to God. It was the beginning of my Christian walk with God.

STUDYING AT IBENGA GIRLS SCHOOL

This book would not be complete if I do not mention about the time I spent at Ibenga Girls secondary School where I spent five years and completed my secondary school education. Ibenga Girls is a secondary Boarding School that has always provided quality education for girls. During my time it was run by the Dominican Sisters under the Catholic Church. It is now currently run by the Franciscan Sisters of Assisi. It is located in the rural Mpongwe District. We had to pass through the dusty road to get to the school. For those students who were using public transport, there was a truck which used to pick up students from what used to be called Saili's shop in Luanshya, one of the small cities in Zambia which was the boundary of Mpongwe District. Since it was an open truck, girls would be almost be covered in dust on arrival at Ibenga. It was fun and an experience. When my dad decided to drive my sister and I to Ibenga, we would then escape that dusty experience. Since we would be there for a whole term, we did lots of shopping of groceries in advance to last for the whole term. These we carried along with our suitcases and bags.

It was my first time to be away from home but I soon adapted to the new environment. It was not difficult as my elder sister Judith had been there for a year before I joined her. We had orientation and were given our uniforms. I remember vividly our brown pleated skirts with white blouses and green jumpers with our white headband. I felt so happy to have passed to go to secondary school, and not only any secondary school, but a much sought after girls boarding school. Once a term began we would not see home until the term ended but parents would come and visit. I was twelve years when I went to Ibenga Girls and I will forever be grateful for the teaching received whilst there because that gave me a good foundation for my Christian Walk.

The Dominican sisters were like our parents away from home. They were committed to bringing up girls that had good morals and disciplined. Of course there would always be bad eggs in every society, but on the whole we were taught well, preparing us for the challenges out there in the world. Among things taught were manners, morals and etiquette. We were also taught responsibility by assigning us different chores from cleaning, gardening, laundry and all household chores. I had also participated in the Adult Literacy Programme where we would go into villages to teach villagers literacy lessons.

When it came to budgeting, I learnt how to budget with my pocket money so that it would last for the term but we would usually receive more money through the post when we needed to top up.

When we were finally ready to leave Ibenga Girls School after successfully completing Year 12 our then Headmistress, Sister De Pache gave us a speech which I will always remember and never forget. That was the year 1972. We had gathered in the assembly hall for her to bid farewell to us when she said and I quote " girls you are now going into the world, soon you will be looking forward to getting married and you will look forward for a better man to marry you. Then she went on to say that in order for you to find a better person, you have to be the better person yourself." I have embraced this principle in every area of my life, whether marriage, work or relationships. I have cherished the input of those dear sisters at Ibenga Girls School for that was the Christian foundation upon which the rest of the building was built.

NDOLA SCHOOL OF NURSNG

As a person who loves people naturally, I had planned to be a nurse while at Ibenga Girls school and therefore applied to the School of Nursing in Lusaka, the capital City of Zambia through the Careers Master in 1972. By March, 1973 I was informed that I had been selected to pioneer the opening of a new School of Nursing in Ndola, the third largest city in Zambia. I informed my dad and mum and in April 1973, I started my nurse training at the Ndola School of Nursing based at Ndola Central Hospital.

When I started the course, I worked hard and passed all examinations and was either in 1st or 2nd place in most examinations. I finished nearly two years and just two months left before entering third year, an uncle who was married to my dad's elder sister passed away and I had to attend the burial. I then got permission from the Vice Principal of the School of Nursing and attended the burial. I had missed my placement for two hours from 2pm to 4pm as I had attended the morning session at a Children's hospital where I was doing my placement. Upon return to the Nursing School, I found a message that the

Principal Tutor wanted to see me in the morning before I left for placement. I went in to see her in uniform ready to go for placement. When I entered her office, I was shocked to hear these words "Florence, because you did not get permission from me to go to the funeral, you have been dismissed from the Nursing School" The pain that I felt is unimaginable, as here was my 22 months training gone just like that. Some people who were dismissed from the Nursing School were either pregnant or failed. But here I was, working hard, passing and only a year to go, my course was terminated. I was devastated but I didn't want to give up easily, therefore I went to the Governor's office to seek for intervention, but all efforts failed until I gave up.

When I was dismissed from the Nursing School, my classmates were very upset and felt I was unfairly treated so much that they displayed their anger in the following incidence: In their third year with four months left to complete the course, one of the students absconded from placement where she was on night duty to go and attend a party for a married couple of two doctors working at the same hospital. The Night Superintendent reported the matter to the Principal Tutor but because it was assumed that the Student Nurse was the Principal Tutor's favourite, she didn't want to dismiss her. The students wrote a petition to the Principal Tutor and said "Florence went to attend a funeral for two hours, you dismissed her. This student went for pleasure for twelve hours and you want to keep her. If you want to keep her then bring Florence back." Unfortunately, the Principal Tutor had no choice but to dismiss her. I felt really bad for her when I heard as she only had four months left to her completion of the course.

THE BEGINNING OF CHALLENGES

Just before I started training at the Nursing School I met my late husband in March 1973 and by October 1974 we had a huge engagement party. Lawrence had agreed with my family that he was going to wait for me to complete my training before getting married. However, as things turned out, he proposed that since I was no longer in training, we should go ahead and get married and then go for another course later because he didn't want me to start another course as it would prolong our engagement. We therefore got married in April 1975 and had our first born daughter in February 1976.

I had a lot of challenges in the first few years of our marriage, though we had a good marriage in the later years. The fact that I didn't complete the course and other challenges opened a door for demonic oppression. I remember being put on sleeping tablets by the doctor due to anxiety and insomnia, which is lack of sleep. My friend Catherine mentioned to me that Bishop Milingo of Lusaka Roman Catholic Church was conducting sessions to pray for people to deliver them from demonic oppression. I therefore travelled to Lusaka, the capital city of Zambia for prayers. I became better for some time but again the problem came back as there was no grounding in the word of God. I was a religious Christian but hadn't experienced the new birth and had not even heard of being born again before.

In Luke 11:24 the word of God says that when an unclean spirit is gone out of a man, he walketh through dry places, seeking rest, and finding none he says, I will return into my house whence I came out and when he findeth it swept and garnished then goeth he, and taketh with him seven other spirits more wicked than himself and they enter in, and dwell there; and the last state of man is worse than the first. What happened was that I had been delivered but because I was not grounded in the Lord demonic oppression resurfaced. I sought several doctors with a lot of hospital appointments with no help. The demonic oppression was such that I would feel like strength was squeezed out of me as I felt like my heart was being squeezed. I would literally feel objects moving in my body. Since the problem was spiritual, the doctors could not identify what was wrong with me. At one point I was referred to see a psychiatrist consultant as the doctors felt that I may have been imagining pain. The thought of being referred to a psychiatrist was devastating. I remember crying in front of the consultant psychiatrist as I explained to him that I was not imagining pain but that the pain and all the body movements in my body were real. The Consultant wrote back to the doctors that I had anxiety. My life had been characterised by so many bad experiences and incidents that I wouldn't know what was coming next. Not only was I afflicted in my body but I passed through so many difficult situations. There was a time when I was so unwell I had to live by the native healer's house for several months as she tried to cast out demons by beating drums. My hair was cut and I had bold head with white beads in my head. This lady was not helping at all as we discovered that she was just playing tricks so that I could stay longer at her place while my husband provided all the groceries for the entire family. My husband had to decide to take me away and told me never to step my feet again at that house. Other experiences I had were snakes and snake bites. One day when my house assistant was off duty I was cleaning the house. We didn't have a hoover at that time so I had just brushed the carpet in the lounge and wanted to move the sofas to the middle of the carpet to enable me clean the sides butI couldn't manage to move the three seater sofa. As I struggled I discovered there was a snake underneath the sofa. I grabbed my daughter who was just under two years and run outside to call neighbours who came and killed the snake. I was lucky my fingers were not bitten as I had placed them under the sofa while pulling. In later years I had been bitten by snakes about three times. This happened that whenever I dreamt a certain relative, the snake would bite me. One snake bite was when I was picking vegetables from the garden. The third bite was very serious. I was at home doing household chores and went outside. Little did I know that there was a snake in the space dividing the water drain from the green lawn area in front of the kitchen which was a few meters from our orchard of guava and mango and mulberry trees.

BACK TO COLLEGE

After feeling a bit better I pulled myself together and decided I needed to go back to college. I therefore applied to go for teaching and was accepted. After being at the Teacher's Training College for a while I was not satisfied that the course was for me, and knew that I was wasting time, therefore I decided to leave after two months. I then decided to apply at the Zambia Institute of Technology to do a Shorthand Typist Course for fifteen months. I had made up my mind that despite what I had gone through I had to be determined and get a qualification. I was not satisfied to be a housewife without a career, I therefore made a journey to go to Kasama, the northern part of Zambia where my mother lived and took my daughter there. I had asked her if she could kindly take care of my daughter while I pursued my course. My loving mother gladly agreed. It was such a big sacrifice for my mother as she was working at that time. She had to add additional duties to her housemaid of baby sitting as well.

After coming back from my mother's place, I went to college and ensured that I worked very hard so that I could pass and qualify to enable me get my daughter back and also get myself a good job. As much as I loved my daughter and wanted to be with her, I had to sacrifice to take her to my mother even though it was far away because I knew that once I had a qualification I could look after my daughter well as at that time things were not going on well in my marriage. I missed her so much during the time she was with my mother. The fifteen months went so quickly as I was quite busy because in addition to the day classes I enrolled myself into the evening class for the same course so that I could stand a chance of passing without fail. I was among the best students of the class as per the Testimonial given to me by the Principal at the college on completion of the course.

NEW JOB

On the last day of the exam in December 1978 I travelled immediately to my mother's place to pick up my daughter as I had missed her very much. Once I came back, I applied for a job as a Secretary and was called for interviews. On the day of interview on 12th January 1979 I did so well that I was given an appointment letter immediately and started work immediately. My interview was in the morning and by 2pm I had started work. I was given the position of Secretary to the Chief Personnel Manager of Administration at ROP (Refined Oil Products), a parastatal company. I worked there for four months only and found a better paying job at the Central Bank of Zambia where I was appointed Secretary to the Deputy Regional Manager. I was among the pioneers of the newly built Regional Office of the Central Bank of Zambia. I was also given the responsibility of interviewing Typists who wanted to join the Bank. I was very happy at the Central Bank because we had very good conditions. I was in middle management and enjoyed perks such as school fees for my children, utility bills , housing and car allowance.

DEMONIC OPPRESSION RESURFACES

While at the Central Bank God blessed us with four more children, bringing the total to five and just when I had my 2nd child, I became sickly again. At one time I had food poisoning so that my child was weaned at four months old as I could not breastfeed her. I managed to survive by God's grace. Even though I was not well, I could still manage to work and go on with my life but was under demonic oppression, which made me unwell most of the time. This went on for several years without help. I also lost so much weight and as doctors would not help since they could not identify the problem, I resorted to native healers but could only get temporal relief and the problems kept on coming back. The native healers used roots or barks or leaves of trees which were given to me to either soak in water and drink, or bath with the same mixtures or steam under a blanket. This went on daily.

When I had my 4th child my predicament became worse. My mother and I and my young child had to travel to a very remote part of the country which was known for its expertise in native medicine. My brother in law was a teacher in that part of the country and he and his wife hosted us but we had to move to the home of the native healer to facilitate easy access to the medicines. They gave us a guest accommodation with was a small grass thatched hut which had a hole in the roof. We had a bit of charcoal fire in one corner to keep us warm and in another corner we perched a mattress on the floor on which my mother, myself and my child slept. My mother said she would sleep by the side near the small grass door to protect my daughter and I from any danger. That is the heart of caring mother. I will forever be grateful to my mother for her determination and commitment to see me well. She left her business to come and care for me. We spent quite a few months without getting better.

I was on unpaid sick leave for five months from my employers Bank of Zambia and they were concerned. They requested that I come back in order for them to see whether they could send me abroad to UK for treatment since we had that facility. My late husband then sent a telegram, as there were no mobile phones at that time. The telegram was to inform me that I should get back home. This had followed the following incidence. One day my baby daughter was sleeping in the little hut and my mother went somewhere. I sat outside on a little stool and gazed at the hut where we used to sleep. I remembered my beautiful home, which I had left to come to this village. I prayed to God the following prayer silently. "Dear God, I know that you are there. I am asking you to heal me of my predicament. When you heal me, I promise that I will serve you for the rest of my life". I said this prayer without opening my mouth but God heard me. It reminds me of Isaiah 65:24 which says before they call I will answer; while they are yet speaking I will hear. God had a different plan for me. It was after this prayer that I received the telegram to go back home. My mother, my daughter and myself started off for home and arrived safely.

GOD SENDS A MESSENGER

Soon after our arrival from the remote village, I was going down the road one day when I met my former neighbour Elizabeth. When Elizabeth was my neighbour she used to be sickly as I was and we used to encourage one another by telling each other where we got the latest concoctions from native healers. She asked me how I was and I told her that I was not well and had just come back from the Northern Province to seek treatment from native healers. Elizabeth looked at me and was moved with compassion. She then told me that she was going to come and see me that coming Sunday.

True to her word she came and told me that she had recovered from her illness, which she had suffered from when she was my neighbour. Since my thoughts were always thinking of native healers, I asked her which native healer healed her so that I could also go there. She replied and said it wasn't a native healer who healed her but Jesus through prayer. I asked her several times whether she didn't take any medicine to which she replied that it was only Jesus through the power of prayer. I was quite puzzled since I had never heard of anyone getting healed without taking medicine. She then said she was going to come back again after a few days.

When she came back she brought along three more people, namely Sister Peggy, Sister Patricia and brother Jairos. They all came from Christian Bible Church. They gave me some words of encouragement from the word of God and prayed for me. They cast out demons that were tormenting me and I noticed that every time a particular demon was cast out, whatever that demon had brought in my body left immediately. I was completely delivered and set free because of Jesus. May His name be glorified.

The word of God in Phillipians 2:9-11 says that there is a name that is above every name and that every knee shall bow and every tongue confess that Jesus is Lord. Indeed because of the redemption in the blood of Jesus and the name of Jesus, I was set free completely as the word of God says in John 8:36 "So if the Son sets you free you shall be free indeed. In Isaiah 55:6 the word of God says "Seek the Lord while he may be found; call on him while he is near. " I sought the Lord while he would be found and called on Him. In Jeremiah 30:17 God said "for I will restore health unto thee and heal thee of thy wounds". He indeed restored my health and healed my wounds.

REPENTANCE AND SALVATION

In 1 John 1:8-9 the bible says "if we say that we have no sin, we deceive ourselves, and the truth is not in us, if we confess our sins, he is faithful and just to forgive us our sins, and to cleanse us from all unrighteousness"

In Romans 3:23 the word of God says "for all have sinned, and come short of the glory of God." I had sinned before God and had to repent of all sins committed in word, deed and thought knowingly and unknowingly. In Isaiah 1:18 the Lord said "come now, let us reason together, though your sins be as scarlet they shall be as white as snow, though they be red as crimson, they will be like wool." God promises in Isaiah 43:25 that He blotteth out our transgressions and will not remember our sins anymore. We are encouraged in Psalms 103:2 that as far as the east is far from the west, so far has He removed our transgressions. What an awesome promise. I accepted the offer and asked Jesus to forgive me and invited Him into my life and was born again. I had not heard anything about being born again before, therefore it was indeed a new experience. However, I was not the only one who had never heard of being born again. In John 3:3 Nicodemus, a Pharisee and ruler in Israel came to Jesus by the night and said unto Jesus " Rabbi, we know that thou art a teacher come from God: for no man can do these miracles that thou does, except God be with him." Jesus answered and said unto him, verily, verily, I say unto thee, Except a man be born again, he cannot see the kingdom of God. Nicodemus said unto Him, how can a man be born when he is old? Can he enter the second time into his mother's womb and be born? Jesus answered " verily, verily, I say unto thee, except a man be born of water and of the Spirit, he cannot enter into the kingdom of God. That which is born of the flesh is flesh and that which is born of the Spirit is spirit."

In Romans 10:9 the bible says "that if thou shalt confess with thy mouth the Lord Jesus, and shall believe in thine heart that God has raised him from the dead, thou shall be saved." I received the Lord Jesus Christ as my Lord and Saviour, the greatest miracle I have ever received. That was the beginning of my real walk with the Lord and I have never looked back ever since. In Romans 10:13 and Acts 2:21 the word of God says "for whosoever calls upon the name of the Lord shall be saved". Jesus said in John 10:10 " the thief cometh not, but for to steal, and to kill, and to destroy; I am come that they might have life, and that they might have it more abundantly." The devil had come to steal my health, my joy my peace, my strength but when Jesus showed up things were different for He restored what the devil stolen. 1 John 3:8 says for this purpose the Son of God was manifested, that He might destroy the works of the devil. So when Jesus came into my life the works of the devil that caused demonic oppression were destroyed glory to Jesus. The shackles of bondage were broken.

Repentance does not end when one accepts the Lord as one's saviour but is a daily process. Many times we sin before God without knowing or even knowingly for none is righteous, not even one the bible says in Romans 3:10. Walking in the light enables us to regularly confess our sins, allowing the blood of the Lord Jesus Christ to continuously cleanse us.

Having gone through repentance and forgiveness of sins that I received from the Lord Jesus Christ through the redemptive power that is in the blood of Jesus which was shed at the cross of Calvary I am now a free person. I accepted my new identity as a new creature in Jesus Christ and now walk in my liberty as a believer. I received a new life through the power of the Holy Spirit and I continue to abide in Christ Jesus by studying and standing on the word of God and praying without ceasing. I now pursue a life that glorifies the Lord and no longer lives in the past. I would like every reader to know that the first thing to do whenever you face any form of challenge is to seek the Lord. I have found joy as a true born again believer than when I was not a believer and I have assurance of eternal life. I can only say "Oh taste and see that the Lord is good."

LIGHT OF THE WORLD

God is light and in him there is no darkness at all. If we say that we have fellowship with him and walk in darkness, we lie, and do not the truth. But if we walk in the light as he is in the light we have fellowship one with another, and the blood of Jesus Christ cleanses us from all sin as written it 1 John 1:7.

In John 8:12 Jesus said I am the light of the world. He that followeth me shall not walk in darkness but have the light of life. Jesus is the saviour of the world and he came to save the world. In John 12:46 Jesus said I am come a light into the world, that whosoever believeth on me should not abide in darkness. Living in darkness is living outside of Jesus. In Isaiah 9:2 the word of God says "the people that walked in darkness have seen a great light: they that dwell in the land of the shadow of death, upon them hath the light shined. Further in Colossians 1:12 says " and giving thanks to the Father, who has qualified you to share in the inheritance of His holy people in the kingdom of light. " In

Colossians 1:13 the word of God says who has delivered us from the power of darkness, and hath translated us into the kingdom of His dear Son.

I am very blessed that I had been transferred from darkness into light, what a glorious and loving God we have.

In John 10:10 the word of God says "the thief cometh not but to steal, and to kill, and to destroy: I am come that they might have life and that they might have it more abundantly, that is, more than adequate, over sufficient, well supplied.

The enemy came to steal my joy, peace, and health but when the Lord Jesus showed up he gave back what the chief thief had stolen. Not only did Jesus restore my joy, peace and health but he gave me eternal life. In John 3:16 the word of God says "For God so loved the world that he gave his only begotten son, that whosoever believeth in him should not perish, but have everlasting life. Jesus came to bind up the broken hearted, to proclaim freedom for the captives and release from darkness, for prisoners to proclaim the year of the Lord's favour, to comfort all who mourn, to bestow on them a crown of beauty for ashes, the oil of joy instead of mourning. Isaiah 61:1

A NEW LIFE

In 2nd Corinthians 5:17 the word of God says that "therefore if anyone is in Christ he is a new creature, old things have passed away, behold all things are become new. I was now a new person, saved by grace, ready to enjoy my freedom from bondage and oppression. As the word of God in John 8:36 declares that if the Son therefore shall make you free, ye shall be free indeed. It was such a good experience, which led me to say to myself "why didn't I know about this all these wasted years". But I believe that the Lord had his own time. I was and I still am not that old person but has become a new creation in Christ with a new set of values, actions and attitudes and destiny. My new identity in Christ enables me to crucify the flesh and seek only that which pleases the father, bringing God's glory in all areas of my life. Jesus had paid the price at the cross of Calvary. Ephesians 2:10 says we are His masterpiece, created unto good works.

The new life I found could not just end up with me. I told every member of my family about Jesus and what He had done for me. I told my workmates and anyone I came in contact with. How could I keep quiet about this miracle of salvation, healing and deliverance that I had received.. Someone out there needed to see what I had seen, someone had to listen and be delivered. It didn't matter what critics of born again Christians said, all I know was I was sick but now was healed and delivered. In John 9 vs 24-25 the person Jesus healed of blindness told the critics of Jesus that all he knew was he was blind but now he could see. It didn't matter what other people thought but his deliverance was all that mattered.

One of the things that change when Jesus comes into your life is your language and how you live your life. My language had changed, my life had changed and this change attracted some people resulting in them giving their lives to Jesus. It did not take long for my late husband to accept Jesus as His Lord and Saviour. How could he resist Him when he had seen such change and transformation this salvation had brought to our household. He experienced such accelerated spiritual growth that soon he was ordained as a Deacon and later as an Elder.

At one point when our pastor had gone to further his studies at the Bible College he was appointed to lead the church for two years. He had such passion for the Lord that he ensured that he applied for a plot to build the church and spearheaded the building himself. I remember him waking up very early in the morning and load drums of water onto our van to be delivered to the church plot before going for work. This enabled the church to move from the School premised where we used to meet into the new building.

The Lord kept on adding more and more souls, which saw a tremendous growth. By the time our dear Reverend, who is late completed his studies and came back from Bible College, the church had doubled in size to God's glory. My late husband had such passion for the Lord that he held on to Jesus and always said that when it was time for him to go to glory he would die praying. The Lord granted his desire as indeed just before he passed on he prayed for me and the children and then breathed his last. A few minutes before he passed on he said that he was going to the Promised Land and could not go back now as he had already been given the number. What a glorious way to go. He actually confirmed having been given the number to enter the Promised Land.

THE WORD OF GOD

The secret of living a victorious life lies in bathing yourself in the infallible word of God daily. The word of God is the manufacturers manual. Just as equipment in our homes have instructions about the product, God has given us the word of God as our guide. As we meditate on the word of God we will be able to walk according to the instruction therein and our lives are balanced emotionally, spiritually, financially and mentally. As we bath in the word of God dirt is removed from our minds like water removes dirt from the body. (Ephesians 5:26). Hebrews 4:12 says the word of God is sharper than a two edged sword it penetrates even to the dividing soul and spirit, joints and marrow, it judges the thoughts and attitudes of the heart.

In John 1:1 the bible says "In the beginning was the Word, and the Word was with God, and the Word was God." Therefore we know that the word of God is God Himself talking to us.

When I accepted the Lord Jesus as my Lord and Saviour, the late Reverand and his wife ensured that I was ground in the word of God. In Luke 11:24-26 the word of God says when the unclean spirit is gone out of a man, he walketh through dry places, seeking rest; and finding none, he saith, I will return unto my house whence I came out. And when he cometh, he findeth it swept and garnished. Then goeth he, and taketh to him seven other spirits more wicked than himself; and they enter in, and dwell there; and the last state of that man is worse than the first.

Therefore in order to guard against further attacks I had to equip myself by abiding in the Lord and studying His word. I had developed a deep hunger and thirst for the word of God as I wanted to know more about God and this new life and my new found joy and hence dedicated myself to studying the word of God.

The word of God brings light, it illuminated my mind and the more I studied the word the hungrier I became. David says in Psalms 42:1 "As the deer panteth for the water so my soul longs after you, you alone are my heart's desire and I long to worship you." The word of God brings healing to the body and comfort to the soul. When you read the word of God with an open heart, it enables you to hear from Him. When I read the word of God I pray for God to give me understanding and revelation. Ephesians 1:17-18 says that the God of our Lord Jesus Christ may give you the spirit and revelation in the knowledge of him, that the eyes of your understanding, being enlightened; that ye may know what is the hope of his calling, and that the riches of the glory of his inheritance in the saints.

The word of God is accurate, which means it is free from error or defect, it is exact and precise.

The word of God is perfect according to Psalms 19:7 which says "the law of the Lord is perfect, converting the soul, the testimony of the Lord is sure, making wise the simple".

The word of God is the wisdom of God. A very powerful respectable man of God I know says that wisdom of God is the Law of God applied accurately to solve any problem you may face, be it marital, financial, or sin, or sickness. 2 Timothy 3:16 says "all scripture is given by inspiration of God, and is profitable for doctrine, reproof, for correction in righteousness. God's will is in the word of God. Faith is activated when we read the word of God. Whether you want to grow spiritually, or be healed in your body or from emotional wounds, or build good relationships, or whether you want to conquer depression and enjoy peace, or be free from bad habits such as addiction, or whether you want career success or a good marriage, or whether you have a wayward child, every problem has a solution in the word of God because God's word does not lie, you can rest on it knowing that it will deliver what it says. In Hebrews 6:13, 16 the word of God says God put a seal on His word so much that whatever He has promised in His word has been sealed with His oath as He sealed His covenant with Abraham. In Psalms 138:2 says God honours His word more than His name. He says He will hasten his word to perform it. (Jeremiah 1:12). In Isaiah 43:26 God asks us to put him in remembrance that is to remind Him of what He has said in His word.

In Colossians 3:16 the word of God says Let Christ's word dwell with you richly and in Joshua 1:8 Joshua was advised that "this book of the law shall not depart out of thy mouth, but thou shall meditate therein day and night, that thou mayest observe to do according to all that is written therein: for then thou shall make thy way prosperous and then thou shall have good success."

.

If for example you do not eat the natural food, you can become malnourished and your body would lack the nutrients required for good health, growth and energy. The person who is continuously malnourished may eventually die of malnutrition. But if you eat healthy food then our bodies will be healthy. The food you eat is digested and absorbed into you every cell in your body so that it becomes part of you and produces the benefits for your health. In the same way you should study the word of God and digest it so that the word is absorbed into your spiritual man so that it becomes part of you and delivers the benefits for your spirit man. If on the other hand one doesn't study and meditate on the word of God, the person may end up with spiritual malnourishment and end up with spiritual death as no nourishment is going into the spirit man. Proverbs 4:20-22 says "My son, attend to my words, incline thine ear to my sayings. Let them not depart from thine eyes; keep them in the midst of thine heart, for they are life unto them that find them and health to their flesh".

Another important reason why you need to study the word of God is that you should know what the word of God says about every problem you encounter. Praying the word is reminding God of what He has said and since He has said and has promised to watch over His word, He is obligated to do what He promised because He cannot lie.. But we can only pray the word if we know the word of God and what it says concerning every situation in our lives. By studying and meditating upon His word. The word of God is a weapon against the devil. Jesus used the word of God to rebuke Satan when he was tempted after fasting for forty days and forty nights. He answered the devil with the word "it is written" and the devil had no power over him as he finally left him (Matthew 4:1-11). Sometimes you may face a very challenging situation be it sickness, marital problem or work or family problem but when you stand on what God has said and speak that word despite how the situation looks like negatively, you will experience victory. You may not remember exactly the scripture where it is written but as long as you keep it in your heart you can withdraw from it whenever it is needed. It is like depositing money into a bank account and be able to withdraw it when needed. You must feed on the word of God, believe, meditate and speak it so that it can work for you. These days you can download free audio bible from the Internet and be able to listen to it at any time of the day if you don't have time to read the hard copy. You can read the hard copy when you create some time because it is important. In Joshua 1:8 God said to Joshua "this book of the law shall not depart out of thy mouth, thou shall meditate therein day and night, that you may observe to do according to all that is written therein, for then thou shall make thy way prosperous, and thou shall have good success".

Many years ago whilst in Zambia, I was feeling unwell and the doctor requested that I do some blood test to check for any clues. When I went back to see him for results, he gave me a negative report about diabetes and immediately I heard the word "let God be truthful and man be a liar" (Romans 3:4), which meant that I had to believe God's report that I was healed two thousand years ago.

BENEFITS OF STUDYING THE WORD OF GOD

The word of God illuminates according to Psalms 19:8 which says "the statutes of the Lord is pure, enlightening the eyes. Psalms 119:105 says "Thy word is a lamp unto my feet and a light unto my path". The word of God is trustworthy, it is dependable and it transforms.

Studying the word of God will enlighten us in knowing the will of God concerning our lives. We will not be at a loss when it comes to decision-making whether it is at home or at work. For example if a married man wants to entice you, you cannot agree, or at work your fellow worker asks you to do something contrary to company rules you will only do what the word says.

Another benefit is that we will not be shaken when we face challenges, as we will remember what the word of God says concerning that matter. If you are sick you know the will of God concerning healing and you would quote 1 Peter 2:24 which says "by His stripes ye were healed". Your faith will be built up as you meditate on the word of God. You will not walk by what you see but by faith irrespective of what the situation looks like in the natural. You will have assurance of the outcome of the matter, knowing that God always leads us in triumph in Christ Jesus (2 Corinthians 2:14-16).

God speaks to us through situations, intuition and his voice among other ways but as mentioned earlier one of the ways He speaks to us is through His word and daily studying and meditating on the word of God helps us recognise His voice when he speaks to us. To know God's voice, you have to spend time with Him in prayer and reading His word. In John 10:27 the word of God says "My sheep hear My voice, and I know them, and they follow Me". The word of God in Isaiah 44:3-5 says I will pour water upon him that is thirsty, and floods upon the dry ground: I will pour my spirit upon thy seed, and my blessing upon thine offspring. In John 6:63 the word of God says " it is the Spirit who gives life; the flesh profits nothing. The words that I speak to you are spirit, and they are life.

Healing is guaranteed when you stand on the word of God. In Proverbs 4:20-22 the word of God says "My son, give attention to my sayings, do not let them depart from your eyes, keep them in the midst of your heart, for they are life unto those that find them, and health to all their flesh"

You have peace even in troubled waters as the word of God ministers to you. Isaiah 26:3 says "thou wilt keep him in perfect peace, whose mind is stayed on thee because he trusteth in thee"

As I continued in prayer and the word I had the benefit of spiritual growth which was so accelerated by the Holy Spirit so much that I was told that I grew faster spiritually than other people who had been born again for many years. What I had gone through for so many years made me hunger and thirst for the word of God. As surely as the deer panteth for the water so my soul longed after God, I wanted to know more and more of the word of God. The word of God says "blessed are those who hunger and thirst for they shall be satisfied. Matthew 5:6 says blessed are those who hunger for righteousness for they shall be filled. In Isaiah 44:3 the word of God says I will pour water upon him that is thirsty, and floods upon the dry ground.

My hunger for truth and the word of God made me thirst and hunger for more revelation and the Lord by His grace taught me and I became stronger and stronger in the Lord. Isaiah 55:6 says "seek the Lord while he may be found, call ye upon Him while he is near". Thank God I was fortunate to call upon the Lord and seek Him and found Him.

ABIDING IN JESUS CHRIST

My vow to the Lord was that if he healed me and delivered me from demonic oppression I would serve Him for the rest of my life. With that promise I needed the Lord to help me as I could not do it on my own. Thankfully Jesus promised and said "but the Holy Spirit, whom the Father will send in My name, He will teach you all things, and will bring to your remembrance all things that I said to you (John 14:26). I could not do it on my own strength but depended and will always depend on the Holy Spirit to help me be the person that God created me to be. The word of God in Zechariah 4: 6 says not by might, nor by power, but my Spirit, saith the Lord of hosts. In Jeremiah 1:5 the word of God says "before I formed you in the womb I knew you, before you were born I sanctified you, I ordained you a prophet to the nations.

Following Jesus meant and still means surrendering myself to His leadership and following His steps to live as an ambassador of Jesus Christ. Following Jesus is a life of commitment, a life of prayer, a life of crucifying the flesh, letting the Spirit of the Living God lead me and guide me. In Galatians 2:20 the word of God says " I am crucified with Christ: nevertheless I live, yet not I but Christ liveth in me, and the life which I now live in the flesh I live by faith of the Son of God, who loved me, and gave himself for me. When your flesh is crucified you will not follow what the carnal mind will dictate to you but what the Holy Spirit desires of you. An example would be when someone does something bad to you the normal carnal reaction is to retaliate, but a crucified life will instead love and pray for enemies as Jesus commanded in Matthew 5:44.

Since I gave my life to Jesus I have had to live a life of surrender, depending totally on the Lord. Jesus said that we are to abide in Him in order to be fruitful in our walk with Him. He demonstrated this in John 15:1-10 when He said "I am the true vine and my father is the husbandsman every branch in me that beareth not fruit he taketh away and every branch that bears fruit he purgeth it, that it may bring forth more fruit. Now you are clean through the word that I have spoken to you. Abide in me, and I in you. As the branch cannot bear fruit by itself, except it abide in the vine, no more can you except ye abide in me. I am the vine ye are the branches; He that abides in me and I in him, the same bringeth forth much fruit, for without me ye can do nothing. If a man abides not in me, he is cast forth as a branch and is withered, and men gather them and cast them into the fire and they are burned. If he abide in me and my words abide in you, ye shall ask what ye will, and it shall be done unto you. Herein is my father glorified that, ye bear much fruit so shall ye be my disciples. As the father has loved me so have I loved ye, so continue ye in my love. If ye keep my commandments, ye shall abide in my love, even as I have kept my father's commandments and abide in His love. Further the Lord Jesus says in verse 16 "Ye have not chosen me, but I have chosen you that ye should go forth and bring forth fruit and that your fruit should remain, that whatsoever ye ask of the Father in my name, he may give it you.

As believers we should bear the fruit of transformed character, in alignment with the character of Jesus Christ who lives in us. The fruits that we bear should be palatable, other people should pick from the branches the fruits and be able to eat and enjoy the fruit. A bitter or sour fruit cannot be enjoyable. If the Holy Spirit lives in us, then we should bear the fruit of love, joy, peace, forbearance, kindness, goodness, faithfulness, self control.

Jesus was telling the disciples to stay connected to Jesus for it is only by staying connected to Him that the life giving love can flow through Him to us, enabling us to bear fruit. In order to stay connected to Jesus and bear fruit we have to obey his commandments, and to know His commandments is to study the word of God. In order to understand clearly His commandments requires constant daily communication with God through prayer, in His presence and reading the word of God. If you have a friend and want to know this friend better, you have to spend time and communicate with them. When you do that you will be assured of knowing their character, weakness and strength, among other things.

Abiding in the Lord means spending time in God's presence, which enables you to know Him better. I enjoy being in His presence and deliberately sets aside time to be in God's presence daily at specific times to be able to hear from God. I would say I am actually addicted to God's presence it is sometimes hard to leave. A powerful man of God has sung a song "I don't want to leave your presence". I can truly testify that when you are addicted to His presence, you will find it hard to leave, as you just want to continue in that atmosphere.

I enjoy to be in God's presence and when my grandchildren come for a weekend sleepover, we spend time together in God's presence so much that when one of them was one day asked at school to write a family tree and write down the hobbies, she put my hobby as "praying all the time". We had a good laugh and when I asked her why she put that she said she couldn't think of any other hobby that I love. Another time she told her auntie who was coming from outside London and was going to visit their home and mine that she should just go to their home because "grandmother is never alone, she is always with God".

A LIFE OF COMMITMENT

The dictionary states that commitment means dedication, devotion, allegiance, loyalty, faithfulness, fidelity, bond. It is a responsibility, an obligation; it is making a commitment that involves dedicating yourself to something or to a cause. Giving my heart to Jesus my Lord and Saviour meant committing myself to His cause, pledging allegiance to Him. Serving the Lord has been my joy. When you find joy you want to share with other people your newfound joy. Jesus said in Matthew 28:19 therefore go and make disciples of all nations, baptising them in the name of the father son and the Holy Spirit. I had vowed to the Lord that I would serve Him for the rest of my life if he healed me and one of the ways I have been committed to Him is to make Jesus known by sharing the message of salvation to whomever I come in contact with as the Lord permits.

As I continued to grow in the Lord, we started having Bible Studies in our home. The Cell group we started soon grew in number as the Lord kept on increasing us till we were 41 members of the Cell group to the extent that there wasn't enough room in our Living room to accommodate more people. People came to hear the message of the Lord Jesus and the sick were prayed for and many received their deliverance and healing. Our neighbours received the Lord Jesus as their saviour. Acts 2:47 says "praising God and having favour with all people. And the Lord added to the church daily such as should be saved" Many people were added to the fellowship to receive healing deliverance and spiritual growth. People passing by our road always saw gathering at our home such that someone came to ask if they could find a faithful employee from our fellowship. We would have people coming in the night seeking prayer and the Lord was with us working miracles. I remember one day while at church praying one lady started manifesting demons and when I was praying for her the demons in her started threatening me that they would come to me if I cast them out. But with the Lord on our side she was set free from demonic oppression and she is now serving the Lord with the husband. She is also a powerful intercessor. Praise Jesus.

PRAYER

It is said that prayer is the first codeless phone God gave us and that there is no congestion, the network is always available. You will never have to be put on hold when you call, there is always an answer waiting for you. Prayer is not just words but it is our spirit making live contact with God's Spirit. It is pouring your heart to the one who has a solution for every problem. The world renown Evangelist Reinhand Bonke says that since life constantly flows from God like light from the sun when we pray we expose ourselves to its rays and sunbathe in the warmth of divine love and absorb His goodness which penetrates to the core of our existence. It is life from heaven. Prayer is the conveyor belt that carries blessings. Prayer is a powerful force that releases heaven's resource upon earth. It is touching heaven to reach earth. Prayer is warfare, which leads to victory.

Prayer is the first thing that I do when I wake up and it is the last thing I do before going to sleep. I pray during the day as and when time allows but I have set time even for five minutes during lunch break. As an intercessor I am addicted to prayer. I cannot do without it.

I love so much to be in God's presence and wouldn't mind spending the whole day in His presence. I can relate to the song one powerful man of God has sang "I don't ever want to leave your presence". Sometimes when I am at home and I set time to pray, I find myself exceeding that time because time flies so much without realising how fast it goes. David in Psalms 5:3 said "My voice shalt Thou hear in the morning, O Lord; in the morning will I direct my prayer unto Thee, and will look up". Prayer is very vital in our lives. As a partner of Benny Hinn Ministries, I received "A Word For Your Day" newsletter from Pastor Benny in which he said that prayer demonstrates our dependence upon God and recognises His ability to meet our needs to do the impossible. In 1 Thessalonians 5:16 the word of God says "pray without ceasing".

Jesus our master prayed. In John 6:15 the word of God says "when Jesus perceived they were about to come and take Him by force to make Him king, He departed again to the mountain by Himself alone. This shows us that Jesus prayed and mostly He went to pray alone as indicated in the word of God. In Acts 2:42 the word of God says " they devoted themselves to the apostle's teaching and to the fellowship, to the breaking of bread and to prayer. The disciples of Jesus knew the importance of prayer. Just after Jesus ascended to heaven the word of God in Acts 1:14 says that "they all joined together constantly in prayer, along with the women, and Mary the mother of Jesus, and with His brothers. This was before the day of Pentecost. Any revival is birthed by prayer.

In order to be an effective Christian you must make prayer a priority of your life. Let it be a habit. To have a successful prayer life you have to be consistent. When you become consistent in prayer you will find that you get so much used to prayer that sometimes you do it effortlessly. Prayer energises and gives strength to go on in life. Breakthroughs are born through prayer, destinies are born through prayer, direction is born through prayer, and wisdom is born through prayer. The list is endless. When Solomon wanted wisdom from God, he prayed and God gave him wisdom. In 1 Kings 3:16-28 he used wisdom make an intelligent decision to decide a matter when two harlots gave birth in the same house and one slept on the baby. Solomon asked for a sword to divide the baby into two and the real mother of the baby restrained him from slaying the baby which proved she was the mother and in the end got her baby back.

Hannah who would not have a child prayed earnestly to God, resulting into the birth of Samuel as the word of God is written In 1 Samuel. As a result he knew God as a growing boy and into manhood and as he recognised God in childhood, he obeyed and prayed to Him and recognised him in manhood as well. If more children are born from praying parents, and brought up in the environment of the house of God, they would hear God's voice clearly and follow Him. According to a statement by E M Bounds, "Praying Samuels come from praying Hannah's, Praying priests come from the house of prayer, and Praying leaders come from praying homes." How powerful.

When I used to work in Bank of Zambia I didn't have a problem with time of prayer since we used to start work at 08.00 hours but when I changed my career and retrained to become a Registered Nurse after opting for Voluntary Early Separation (VESS) I used to work in hospital and I needed to wake up very early in the morning and prepare to start work at 07.15 hours. This was after coming to UK where I trained at City University, London. One day I said to the Lord, "father you know how I love to pray and be in your presence, please give me a job where I can have enough time to pray in the morning before going to work. God scheduled a situation where my back and leg started hurting so bad that I could no longer work in hospital and was discharged for incapacity after being off sick for ten months. The word of God in Romans 8:28 says "And we know that all things work together for good for them who are the called according to his purpose. At that time it looked quite bad as I wasn't sure what I was going to do. The discharge from work triggered other situations, which only God could solve. Since I was on a Work Permit at that time it meant that my Permit was curtailed as a result of incapacity. But the Lord God came through in the end as He always does. God answered my prayer and gave me a job, which enabled me to have a good time to be in God's presence before I go for work starting at 09.00hrs or 10.00hours

In order to develop a time of prayer, make prayer time as an appointment with God and set time when you pray. You can start with 5 minutes initially and then gradually increase the time on a weekly basis and in no time you will find that you are addicted to prayer. Pray daily because every day you go without prayer you document pride. You tell God you want to be independent, you do not need him, you can figure out yourself what you need.

Discipline yourself and commit yourself to prayer for a certain period of time until a habit is formed. While praying, do not allow distractions. Sometimes thoughts come up as you pray but stay focused. If a phone rings ignore it until you finish praying. Select a place where you pray. If you have enough space in your house you can chose a room where you pray and call it "your secret place". Psalms 91:1 says He who dwells in the secret place of the almighty shall abide under the shadow of the almighty. Sanctify this place and keep a bible and a note pad to write anything God ministers to you. The disciples called their secret place "the Upper Room". Something happens when you get into God's presence, your fears disappear, faith comes, strength comes to overcome every battle,

Jesus taught his disciples to pray what is known as "Our Father prayer in Matthew 6:9-13. It covers asking God for provisions, forgiveness, protection, praise. Knowing how to pray is very important to ensure answers to prayer. Some prayers are not answered because of praying wrongly. We should always start with adoration and praise as in Psalms 100:4 we are told to enter God's presence with praise. Proclaim who He is, Jehovah-Shalom, our peace, Jehovah Jairah our provider, Jehovah Rophe, our healer,Jehovah-Tsidikenu, our righteousness, Jehovah Nissi, our banner, Jehovah-Rohi, our shephered, Jehovah-Elshaddai, our all sufficient God, Jehovah-Sabaoth, the Lord of hosts. You declare that he is your healer, your deliverer and miracle worker.

After adoration and praise follows confession. We should ask God for forgiveness of all sins committed, knowingly or unknowingly. In Psalms 66:18-20 the word of God says "if I regard iniquity in my heart, the Lord will not hear" Why would I pray a prayer that is going nowhere, it is not worth it as it is time wasting. We should follow with thanks giving of what God has done and is doing in our lives, and to thank him for who he is in our lives and then followed by supplication where we present our requests from God and always pray in the name of Jesus. When you pray stand on scripture and remind God of what he has said concerning every problem. Pray scripture that is why it is important to study the word of God because that is where you withdraw when you pray.

The benefits of prayer are that it documents your dependence of God and not on your ability. Prayer is conversation with God and it is a way of telling God to intervene in the affairs of man. It is a platform to communicate with God telling him all our concerns and confess your sins. Through prayer you enter into the Holy of Holies to touch the throne of grace to obtain mercy and find grace in time of need. (Hebrews 4:16) Prayer gives you peace knowing that you have presented your desires to him. God desires that we call on him to enable him answer your prayers. (Jeremiah 33:3). Prayer enables you to draw near to God so that He can draw near to you. (James 4:8). Prayer gives you a platform to thank God for His goodness, His provision and all He has done in your life. Prayer gives peace. Phillipians 4:6 encourages you not to worry but submit your requests to God. Prayer gives strength and comfort in time of need and distress. It gives you boldness and confidence in God giving you assurance that God will answer your prayers. Through prayer you recharge your batteries and receive electricity into our being. Prayer changes things. You can tell God your secrets and he will not disclose to anyone.

There are different positions of prayer. You can pray lying on your bed as it is written "Let the saints be joyful in glory: let them sing aloud upon their beds. (Psalms 149:5)

You can pray on your knees as it is written " For this reason I kneel before the Father, from whom every family in heaven and on earth derives its name." Ephesians 3:14-15). You can pray standing as per what Jesus said " And when ye stand praying, forgive, if ye have ought against any: that your Father also which is in heaven may forgive you your trespasses."(Mark 11:25).

THE HOLY SPIRIT

After accepting the Lord as my Lord and Saviour, I continued learning more about God. However, the part, which I couldn't understand, was receiving the Holy Spirit and speaking in tongues. Whenever we gathered to pray and people started speaking in tongues, I used to wonder how possible was that. I had told my auntie who also gave her life to the Lord at the same time with me that I would just continue worshiping God in truth but not speaking in tongues but as time went on I read the word of God and started understanding what it says about the Holy Spirit. In church one day they asked those who wanted to receive the gift of speaking in tongues to go to the alter. I was among those prayed for but at that time I didn't speak in tongues. One day as we gathered together for Bible Study and prayer I just found myself speaking in tongues as I could not hold my tongue. It was an amazing experience.

Jesus said in Acts 1:8 "But ye shall receive power, after that the Holy Ghost is come upon you: and ye shall be witnesses unto me both in Jerusalem, and in all Judaea, and in Samaria, and unto the uttermost part of the earth. "In Acts 2:2-4 says that when the day of Pentecost came, they were all together in one place.

Suddenly a sound like the blowing of a violent wind came from heaven and filled the whole house where they were sitting. They saw what seemed like tongues of fire that separated and came to rest on each of them. All of them were filled with the Holy Spirit and began to speak in other tongues as the Spirit enabled them. After studying what the word of God says about the Holy Spirit, I came to understand the presence of the Holy Spirit into a believer's life and what He does.

The Holy Spirit is the third person of the Trinity, equal with the father and the Son. He is not an "it" nor wind but a person who desires to have an intimate relationship with us.

The Holy Spirit is the Spirit of knowledge. He is all knowing and reveals secret things. 1 Corinthians 2:9-10 says that as it is written, eye has not seen, nor ear heard, neither have entered into the heart of man, the things that God has prepared for those who love Him. But God has revealed them unto us by His Spirit.

The Holy Spirit is a teacher who teaches us all things. Jesus said in John 14:26 "but the comforter, who is the Holy Spirit whom the father shall send in my name, He shall teach you all things and bring all things to your remembrance all that I said unto you"

The Holy Spirit is our counsellor whom Jesus promised will be with us for ever. John 14:16. Therefore when we, as believers put our trust in Jesus Christ, the Holy Spirit indwells us permanently. 1 Corinthians 3:16 says "know ye not that ye are the temple of God, and that the Spirit of God dwelleth in you".

The Holy Spirit is the source of power which enables us to serve the Lord, witness for the Lord, to have fruit in our lives and also to overcome the devil and his works as written in Acts 1:8.

The Holy Spirit is our prayer partner because he intercedes for us. In Romans 8:26-27 the word of God says "likewise the Spirit also helpeth our infirmities: for we know not what we should pray for as we ought: but the Spirit itself maketh intercession for us with groanings which cannot be uttered. And he that searcheth the hearts knoweth what is the mind of the Spirit because he maketh intercession for the saints according to the will of God.

The Holy Spirit testifies of Jesus Christ. In John 15:26 Jesus said " But when the Comforter is come, whom I will send unto you from the father, even the Spirit of truth which proceedeth from the father, he shall testify of me".

The Holy Spirit abides with us forever as Jesus said in John 14:15-18 "If ye love me, keep my commandments. And I will pray the Father and he shall give you another Comforter, that he may abide with you forever, even the Spirit of truth. The world cannot accept him, because it neither sees him nor knows him.

But you know him, for he lives with you and will be in you. I will not leave you comfortless I will come to you.

The Holy Spirit guides. Romans 8:14 says "for as many as are led by the Spirit of God, they are the sons of God.

The Holy Spirit sends workers and will direct you to the geographical area of your assignment Acts 13:4 says "So they being sent forth by the Holy Ghost departed unto Seleucia and from thence they sailed to Cyprus".

The Holy Spirit commands and reveals to you whom you are assigned to, whether a person, a group, a community or a nation, as written in Acts 8:29 "Then the Spirit said unto Phillip, Go near and join yourself to this chariot"

The Holy Spirit will reveal to you things in your future as written in John 16:13b. " He will shew you things to come."

The Holy Spirit will speak with you and reveal to you your specific assignment, what you are meant to be, whom God has called you to be. Acts 13:2 says "As they ministered to the Lord, and fasted, the Holy Ghost said, Separate Me Barnabas and Saul, for the work whereunto I have called them". That is why it is a dangerous thing for one to do the work which God has not assigned you to do.

Without the Holy Spirit we are lost as Jesus said "without me you can do nothing".John 15:5.

The Holy Spirit desires that we have a conversation with Him. He longs for us to be in His presence. He longs to give us direction, He is the Spirit of Wisdom, knowledge and He wants to impart this to us. We cannot have fellowship with Him unless we have surrendered our lives to Him. Ephesians 1:13-14 says that believers are sealed with the Holy Spirit who is a deposit guaranteeing our inheritance until the redemption of those who are God's possession to the praise of his glory". God has promised eternal life to all those who believe in Jesus Christ and has sent the Holy Spirit to indwell the believer until the day of redemption. In John 14:16, Jesus said the father will give another helper who will be with us forever. Romans 8:9 says that if anyone does not have the Spirit of God in them, they are not saved. If one is saved on the other hand, they should have the indwelling presence of the Holy Spirit. In 1 Samuel 16:14 the Spirit of the Lord departed from Saul but came upon David. After Pentecost the permanent indwelling of the Holy Spirit is God's promise to never leave us nor forsake us. It is possible though to quench the Holy Spirit and grieve Him. Unconfessed sin can hinder our fellowship with God and quench the Holy Spirit working in our lives. It is imperative that all sins are confessed in order for God to cleanse us from all unrighteousness. (1 John 1:9). Therefore even though the

Holy Spirit can never leave us, the benefits and joy of His presence can depart if we live in sin.

We need to cultivate an atmosphere in our lives where we are conscious of the presence of the Holy Spirit at all times. The presence of the Holy Spirit in our lives is the presence of the Lord. Psalms 16:11 says in His presence there is fullness of joy and at His right hand there are pleasures for ever more. The Holy Spirit is the one who brings the intimacy of the love of Jesus Christ to us because in Romans 5:5 the word of God says God has poured out His love into our hearts by the Holy Spirit who was given to us, meaning we cannot love God without the Holy Spirit. In John 15:15 Jesus told His disciples that he called them friends, not servants. The Holy Spirit desires that we be friends. Psalms 139 says " where can I go from your spirit or where can I flee from your presence? If I ascend into heaven, you are there; if I make my bed in hell behold you are there. If I take the wings of the morning, And dwell in the uttermost parts of the sea, even there your hand shall lead me, and your right hand shall hold me. If I say "surely the darkness shall fall on me; indeed the darkness shall not hide from you." We cannot run away from His presence because he is always there. He will never leave us nor forsake us according to Deuteronomy 31:6.

Dependence on the Holy Spirit and His guidance is not something done in a moment but is learned when we practice it continually. A Christian should be open and receptive to the leading and prompting of the Holy Spirit. This gift is not only reserved for preachers and only those who are very spiritual but to all who will take time to listen to Him.

THE HOLY SPIRIT AND TONGUES

One of the evidences of the presence of the Holy Spirit in your life is speaking in tongues. Speaking in tongues is the initial evidence among the many gifts given by the Holy Spirit. 1 Corinthians 12:4-11 says " Now there are diversities of gifts, but the same Spirit and there are differences of administrations, but the same Lord.

And there are diversities of operations, but it is the same God, which worketh all in all.

But the manifestation of the Spirit is given to every man to profit withal.

For to one is given by the Spirit the word of wisdom; to another the word of knowledge by the same Spirit;

To another faith by the same Spirit; to another the gifts of healing by the same Spirit;

To another the working of miracles; to another prophecy; to another discerning of spirits; to another divers kinds of tongues; to another the interpretation of tongues:

But all these worketh that one and the selfsame Spirit, dividing to every man severally as he will.

Speaking in tongues is the language of the Spirit which gives you access to the realm of the Spirit which is the supernatural realm of God. As mentioned earlier in Romans 8:26-27 the word of God says "Likewise the Spirit also helpeth our infirmities: for we know not what we should pray for as we ought: but the Spirit itself maketh intercession for us with groanings which cannot be uttered. And he that searcheth the hearts knoweth what is the mind of the Spirit, because he maketh intercession for the saints according to the will of God." Therefore the Holy Spirit prays through you and bypasses your mind when you pray in tongues. There are problems which you can't even utter and pray about but the Holy spirit takes over by groanings, interpreting your thoughts. Speaking in tongues deepens your prayer life and anointing comes on you. Speaking in tongues builds your spirit man and reaches to the root of your problem. When you speak in tongues only God understands and satan does not understand.

I have experienced situations where my deepest prayer need could not be uttered but would lay down on the floor and not be able to say a word in prayer but just groanings and I have found breakthroughs when I pray this way. Some of the benefits of speaking in tongues is that it enables you to pray on target and takes you into deep things of God. 1 Corinthians 14:2 says "For he that speaketh in an unknown tongue speaketh not unto men, but unto God: for no man understandeth him; howbelt he speaketh mysteries"

When you don't know how to pray over some situation, pray in tongues while focussing on that problem. I remember the story of one powerful woman of God who came to speak at our conference. She told us that many years ago she had a heart problem. One day she prayed in tongues for a continuous two hours and sweated whilst praying. By the time she finished praying she was healed. Another lady told of a story of how one day her daughter was kidnapped and even though she didn't know then what had happened, she was prompted to speak in tongues only to hear that the time she had started praying in tongues that was the time her daughter was kidnapped but was saved by the lord.

If you desire to speak in tongues, ask God to give you as James 1:5 "If any of you lack wisdom, let him ask of God, that giveth to all men liberally, and upbraideth not; and it shall be given him."

HEARING GOD'S VOICE

Many people have asked how can one hear God's voice. Does He speak, can you hear Him. The answer is "yes". It is possible to hear God speak. You have to be connected to His frequency to hear Him speak. Let us put it this way. If your neighbour has SKY or other satellite connections, which enable them, watch different programmes on TV and you have not connected to the same channels, you cannot access and watch the same programmes as your neighbour. Hearing God requires that you connect with Him, it requires intimacy with Him. It requires that you communicate and spend time with Him.

Waking with God is to be aware of his presence every moment of your life. It means listening to Him. God is a Spirit and He speaks to us through the Holy Spirit who dwells within us. God the father, Jesus and the Holy Spirit are one. Jesus said in John 14:19-20 " Before long, the world will not see me anymore, but you will see me. Because I live, you also will live. On that day you will realize that I am in my Father, and you are in me, and I am in you.

Jesus said that He would not leave us as orphans. He said "But ye shall receive power, after that the Holy Ghost is come upon you which is what led to Pentecost. (Acts 1:8).

In John 14:8 Phillip had asked the Lord to show them who the father was and Jesus answered him in verse 10 "Don't you believe that I am in the Father, and that the Father is in me? The words I say to you I do not speak on my own authority. Rather, it is the Father, living in me, who is doing his work. Believe me when I say that I am in the Father and the Father is in me." Therefore we know that when the Holy Spirit speaks, God is speaking to us because they are one. In order to hear God speak you have to be in His presence.

We live in the dispensation of time where we are blessed to hear God speak through the Holy Spirit directly. Hebrews 1:-2 says "In the past God spoke to our ancestors through the prophets at many times and in various ways, but in these last days He has spoken to us by his Son, whom he appointed heir of all things, and through whom also he made the universe." In God's presence we can hear his voice.

In the Old Testament only the high priest could enter into the presence of God called the Holy of Holies and offer sacrifices of blood of animals on behalf of himself and the congregation. They could only enter once a year on the Day of Atonement. God's presence was shielded by a veil, which separated the Holy of Holies from the Holy Place. The Jerusalem Temple was a replica of the wilderness tabernacle and had a long curtain. When Jesus died this curtain was torn in half exposing the Holy of Holies, which meant that God's presence was now accessible to all through the atonement of our sins through His blood at the cross of Calvary. No more animal offerings as the greatest offering had been sacrificed.

Exodus 33:9 says "And it came to pass, as Moses entered into the tabernacle, the cloudy pillar descended, and stood at the door of the tabernacle, and the Lord talked to Moses." Hebrews 10:19-20 says "Having therefore, brethren to enter into the holiest by the blood of Jesus, by a new and living way which he hath consecrated for us through the veil, that is to say, his flesh.

We are blessed to access God's presence any time and communicate with him. If we learn to depend on Him and hear His voice, we cannot go wrong. Isaiah 30:21 says "And thine ears shall hear the word behind thee saying, this is the way, walk ye in it, when ye turn to the right hand, and when ye turn to the left."

God created us to hear his voice and to guide us. In Deuteronomy 4:36 the word of God says "Out of heaven he made thee to hear his voice, that he might instruct thee: and upon earth he shewed thee his great fire; and thou heardest his words out of the midst of the fire.

We have many examples in the bible, which talks about God's people hearing his voice. When Abraham sent his servant to find a wife for his son, he assured him "The God of heaven, who took me from my father's house, and from the land of my kindred and which spake unto me saying unto thy seed will I give this land, he shall send his angel before thee, and thou shall take a wife unto my son from thence."

Another example is in Exodus 33:11a which says "And the Lord spake unto Moses face to face as a man speaketh unto his friend". Further Exodus 6:13a says "And the Lord spake unto Moses and Aaron and gave them a charge unto the children of Israel..

When we seek God and pray, he answers and does speak to us concerning our requests. When you need to make a decision concerning a matter, God will speak to you what needs to be done. We read in 2 Samuel 2:1 "And it came to pass after this that David enquired of the Lord, saying shall I go up unto any of the cities of Judah? And the Lord said unto him Go up." When David further asked God where he must go, God answered him and told him to go to Hebron.

Noah walked with God and God spoke to him and he obeyed his voice. Genesis 6:13 says "And God said unto Noah, The end of all flesh is come before me; for the earth is filled with violence through them; and, behold, will destroy them with the earth."

The word of God tells us in 1 Samuel 3:11 "And the Lord said to Samuel, Behold, I will do a thing in Israel, at which both the ears of every one that heareth it shall tingle."

One of the pre requisites of hearing God's voice is walking in the Spirit. Walking in the spirit is living a lifestyle God's way crucifying the flesh, embracing God's presence. In Galatians 5:16-18 says "This I say then, Walk in the Spirit, and ye shall not fulfil the lust of the flesh. For the flesh lusteth against the Spirit, and the Spirit against the flesh: and these are contrary the one to the other: so that ye cannot do the things that ye would. But if ye be led of the Spirit, ye are not under the law. Romans 8:14 says "for as many as are led by the Spirit of God, are the sons of God."

The bible explains further in Galatians 5:19-21 "Now the works of the flesh are manifest, which are these; Adultery, fornication, uncleanness, lasciviousness, idolatry, witchcraft, hatred, variance, emulations, wrath, strife, seditions, heresies, envyings, murders, drunkenness, revellings, and such like: of the which I tell you before, as I have also told you in time past, that they which do such things shall not inherit the kingdom of God". On the other hand the word of God says in verse 22-26: "But the fruit of the Spirit is love, joy, peace, longsuffering, gentleness, goodness, faith, Meekness, temperance: against such there is no law. And they that are Christ's have crucified the flesh with the affections and lusts. If we live in the Spirit, let us also walk in the Spirit. Let us not be desirous of vain glory, provoking one another, envying one another."

In Revelation 1:10 John wrote "I was in the Spirit on the Lord's Day and I heard behind me a loud voice as of a trumpet." This confirms to us that in order to hear the voice of God you have to be in the Spirit, aligning your spirit with the Spirit of God.

In Genesis 3:8 the bible says about Adam and Eve "And they heard the voice of the Lord God walking in the garden in the cool of the day and Adam and his wife hid themselves from the presence of the Lord God amongst the trees of the garden". This brings us to conclude that sin separates from the presence of the Lord.

As can be seen from the experiences of the men of God in biblical times one can hear the audible voice of God. When the Holy Spirit speaks there are a lot of advantages when that happens. What I give in these passages are not exhaustive but part of my experiences and you will explore your own experiences when you walk with God.

I have cultivated an atmosphere where I am conscious of His presence all the time. I have such a personal relationship with the Holy Spirit such that if I am thinking about something in a different way from the way the situation actually is, I hear the Holy Spirit say "not what you are thinking about Florence. He corrects me instantly.

Sometimes the Holy Spirit grieves. In Hosea 5:15 the bible says " I will go and return to my place, till they acknowledge their offence, and seek my face: in their affliction they will seek me early." The Holy Spirit will withdraw his presence when he is offended. One day I entered church and I saw people lifting up their hands in worship when all of a sudden I felt the Holy Spirit grieving and I asked the Holy Spirit why He was grieving and He said that they worship me with their mouth but their heart is far from me. (Matthew 15:8.) We are instructed not to grieve the Holy Spirit. Ephesians 4:29-32 says "Let no corrupt communication proceed out of your mouth, but that which is good to the use of edifying, that it may minister grace unto the hearers. And grieve not the holy Spirit of God, whereby ye are sealed unto the day of redemption. Let all bitterness, and wrath, and anger, and clamour, and evil speaking, be put away from you, with all malice: And be ye kind one to another, tender-hearted , forgiving one another, even as God for Christ's sake hath forgiven you."

I love the presence of the Lord and I do not allow anything that would grieve Him. I depend on Him daily and cannot afford any time without his presence. He is my compass who directs me where to go. He reveals secret things and warns me of events ahead of time and even any impending danger. John 16:13 says "Howbeit, when the Spirit of truth is come, he will guide you into all truth, for he shall not speak of himself; but whatsoever he shall hear, that he shall speak, and he will show you things to come.

Many instances the Holy Spirit has instructed me to pray and avert disaster. One time while still in Zambia, one of the businesses I had was rearing chickens and eggs for sale. One day as my house assistant and my garden assistant and the children were helping me dressing chickens to get them ready to fulfil customer orders, I heard the Holy Spirit tell me to stop what I was doing and go in the house to pray. I told the Holy Spirit that my usual time for intercession was 9pm. As intercessors we had 24 hour prayer rota where each prayer warrior had to select a time suitable for them to pray as we interceded on various issues. Every week we had a list of prayer items circulated. Sometimes my time of prayer would be at 0200 but that month I was interceding at 9pm that is why I told the Holy Spirit that my time was 9pm but the Holy Spirit told me to go and pray at 12 noon. I obeyed and immediately entered my bedroom and checked on the Prayer list for that day. The list indicated that we were praying against armed robbers among other prayer items. I found myself crying out to the Lord to protect my husband. After a while I went back to continue dressing chickens and then the land phone rang. My youngest daughter answered but the line got cut. She thought that someone may have been be playing with the phone but I told her to let me answer next time it rings. When it rang next I answered and it was a nurse from Casualty Department at the hospital who asked me whether I was Mrs Mponda to which I agreed. She then went on to advise me that my husband had been attacked by armed robbers and the car had been stolen at gunpoint but that my husband was injured but survived. Therefore if I didn't obey the Holy Spirit to pray the story would have been different.

One time my youngest son was going to school in the morning but before he went I was telling him about the power in the name of Jesus and that he should call on Him all the time My son asked "mum even on the road" to which I agreed. We prayed and he went to school. I continued praying and heard the voice of the Holy Spirit asking me to call him. I said to myself that my son would not be happy because the school confiscated phones that rang in class as I was assuming he was already in class. I didn't call and the next thing was the school rang and advised me that my son had just been hit by a car, they called the ambulance and by the time my eldest son and I drove to school, the ambulance crew was attending to him. It happened that when my son and his friend were walking to school, his friend decided he would go through the park while my son used the main road. His friend met a dog in the park and he was running back to the road he was just in time as he saw my son being hit by a car, lifted up in the air turned three times and fell down on the curb but he didn't hit his head on the curb because his friend had laid his hands and caught him before hitting his head down. When later he was seen by the doctor, the doctor said in his six years working in Accident and Emergency, he had never seen anything like that where a person was hit by a car, lifted up in the air, turned three times and the doctor said it was indeed a miracle. That is the power of prayer.

Another incidence was one Saturday my son told me he was going for a party. Since it was around 8pm I told him that I would give him 2 hours to attend the party to which he agreed. Before he went I heard the Holy Spirit tell me I should pray for him and anoint him. I quickly told him to come back and after praying for him and anointing him, he left but even though he left I still had a burden to pray for him and continued praying. As I prayed non stop, my youngest daughter came rushing to me that my son was badly attacked and injured and was rushed to hospital by ambulance. The kind lady whose son went quickly to save my son on the road and took him in the house while the attackers ran away called my daughter. She covered him as he was in shock due to bleeding and cared for him before the ambulance arrived.

We quickly jumped into the car and drove to the hospital. We were asked by a policeman to wait in a room while the doctors attended to him. The policeman came to inform us that his lung was pierced but fortunately the heart was intact.

If I didn't obey the voice of the Holy Spirit to pray, the story would have been different but thank God I obeyed.

One night some years ago whilst still I Zambia I was at home with my children as my late husband was working out of town. when I heard the Holy Spirit say "cover all your children with the blood of Jesus". I immediately obeyed and prayed for my children. A few minutes later there was a knock on the front door. We asked who it was and my cousin's wife was at the door with her baby daughter down with measles, an infectious disease. My cousin was away for training in UK. She had travelled from another part of town to come so that I could pray for the daughter. I prayed for her and commanded the measles to dry up in the name of Jesus and also decreed that none of my children would get measles. By the following day the baby was fine and none of my children got the disease. What an awesome God He is.

While working at Bank of Zambia, one of the Directors in the Legal department at Head office passed away. A few of us were selected to represent the Regional Office at the funeral. Due to some delays we didn't start off during the day but started off around 7pm. The driver passed through the Service Station to fill gas. As we were in the land cruiser, the Holy Spirit asked me to pray. I asked everyone could pray and I led the prayers. Just as we joined the main road we were nearly involved in an accident but the Lord preserved us and the Personnel Officer who was a believer like me just commented "the power of prayer". God warns of dangers ahead of time.

Whilst still in Zambia one night my youngest daughter and I went for an all night prayer at my church, Assemblies of God. Around 4am my daughter felt very cold and wanted to go back home. I was the Vice chairperson for the intercessory team so I told the Chairperson that I was taking my daughter home. As I drove, passing over the bridge over a river I saw a lot of dust covering the whole area of the bridge.

Many years ago while in Zambia I had diagnosed with Diabetes. As most people know it is not a good condition and was believing God for healing. One day in my prayer time the Lord showed me a vision of the pool of Bethsda where Jesus healed the man who had an infirmity for thirty eight years. An angel of the Lord would at a certain time stir up the water in the pool and whoever went in first would be made whole of the infirmity. (John 5:1-8). The Lord assured me that when the water was stirred up, I would be made whole. I didn't understand the meaning so I asked the Lord where would I find the pool and He told me that He would be sending his servant to hold a crusade and that I should attend this crusade and when the Holy Spirit moved I should surrender myself totally at that moment and I would be made whole.

The man of God came from South Africa named Peter Pretorious and my church was involved in helping out at the crusade. I told my pastor what the Lord had told me and he encouraged me. My late husband and I attended the crusade and as the Lord said, the man of God told us that the Holy spirit was moving and that each one of those believing God for healing should touch the place where they needed healing. I touched my body as requested and by the following day I felt different. A few days later I had a review with the consultant who told me my blood sugars had gone back to normal and he asked me what happened. I then told him that I went for prayers. When I developed high blood pressure later in the coming years the Lord gave me instructions of what to do and when I followed the instructions, I was healed of high blood pressure and was stopped taking medication by the doctor.

As mentioned earlier, the Holy Spirit speaks, guides and sends. I have a principle in my life that I need to pray and ask the Lord about everything. In Exodus 33:13-15 we see that Moses asked God to show him God His way and God spoke to Moses that he would go with him. Moses told God that he would not go without God's presence. As for me, I cannot even change locations unless I have heard clearly from the Lord. For example my coming to UK was not decided by me but by the Lord Himself. He spoke to me through dreams and confirmations as Daniel 2:19 says "then the secret was revealed unto Daniel in a night vision". Before coming to UK I asked the Lord to lead me to the right church where the Lord would want me planted. My son eldest son and I attended a church on our first Sunday in the UK which was near where we lived but my spirit didn't settle for that church. My daughter told me she goes to KICC (Kingsway International Christian Center) in London and would take us when she was off and when we went to KICC I felt at peace and later had a dream KICC was like an umbrella and confirmed by our pastor in one of his sermons.

It was soon after giving my life to the Lord and having a great desire to know the Lord, the Lord started revealing things to me through visions and dreams and hearing His voice. In Acts 2:17 the word of God says "And it shall come to pass in the last days, saith God, I will pour out of my Spirit upon all flesh: and your sons and your daughters shall prophesy, and your young men shall see visions, and your old men shall dream dreams. When I had the first vision, even though I cannot recall exactly what it was, I quickly opened my eyes as I got scared what I started seeing like a film. You will understand that I had not known or seen anything like that in my life so I quickly opened my eyes and after prayers I told my sisters in Christ what I saw and then pastor explained to me that I had just seen a vision. From then onwards the Lord would reveal to me a lot of things.

One day we had been trusting God for release of foreign exchange by Bank of Zambia to enable Pan African Women Alliance women attend a conference in Malawi. I suddenly saw a gush of dollars come and being allocated to each one of us that were travelling which signified that the dollars had been released. Another case was one sister in the Lord who had been having caesarian section for her pregnancies and was expecting a third pregnancy. The Lord opened my eyes as we prayed and saw that the Lord was expanding her pelvis. I told everyone what I had seen and truly as the Lord had revealed to me she gave birth in the normal way.

THE LORD JESUS APPEARS TO ME

Talking about the second coming of the Lord Jesus Christ the word of God says in Revelation 1:7 "Behold he cometh with clouds; and every eye shall see him, and that also which pierced him, and all kindreds of the earth shall wail because of him. Even so. Amen". Again the word of God in Mark 13:25-26 says "And the stars of heaven shall fall, and the powers that are in heaven shall be shaken. And then shall they see the Son of man coming in the clouds with great power and glory."

I spent one evening worshiping and went to bed like any other night. Then I had a dream that I was in church and our Resident pastor, Pastor Yemisi Ashimolowo was preaching. All of a sudden I realised in the dream that the position where I was sitting had changed and realised that the church now was transformed into a very big ship and it was cruising at very high speed. I changed position and then realised that there were clouds in front of me, literally I was staring in the clouds. As I was wondering what that meant, thought that may be I was going to heaven when I suddenly saw Jesus Christ appear in those clouds and had his stretched arms. I could see clearly his pierced hands as He stretched his hands. Then suddenly a friend who had come to visit came into the bedroom and woke me up. I started telling her Jesus had just appeared to me. Later that morning I went to see my newly born granddaughter to help my daughter bath her. After that before leaving I was praying and just as I closed my eyes I could see in a vision that I had stars glittering around my face. I then proceeded to church for Wednesday Bible Study and midweek service. After the service I met with a sister in the Lord who belonged to the Home cell group I went to and since I was very excited, shared the dream. Then she said and I quote "sister Florence I know you are always glowing but today you have a different glow on your face."

Then another day I was by the dining room speaking with a sister in the Lord on the phone when I suddenly saw an angel appear at the door, which leads to the hallway, and I immediately told the sister that I was going to call her later. I followed the angel and he led me to my bedroom where I knelt down on my knees and started worshiping the Lord. After being in worship for a while I stood up and lay on my bed. For the second time I just saw the clouds again and the lord Jesus appeared to me again. This time I was not dreaming but it was like I was in a trance. The scars in His hands were very vivid. It was such a glorious experience.

ANGELIC ENCOUNTERS

The Holy Spirit speaks with us through the word of God, circumstances, pastors and priests, other believers and through angels. He speaks to us through dreams, visions other gifts of the Holy Spirit like prophesy.

Angels are supernatural beings created by God to execute orders as the Holy Spirit directs. There are different types of angels such as praise angels, worship angels, ministering angels, and warring angels. Their highest purpose is to exalt the name of Jesus. Angels are real. They are not imaginary. Whether you have seen angels or not they are real and they are sent by God to minister to His people. Sometimes God opens people's eyes and allows angels to manifest themselves in physical form as revealed in Genesis 32:1-2 which says "And Jacob went on his way and the angels of God met him. And when Jacob saw them, he said "this is God's host and he called the name Mahanaim". In Luke chapter 1 the angel introduced himself to Zacharia, the priest that he was Gabriel that stands in the presence of God and that he was sent to speak unto him to show him the glad tidings that his wife Elizabeth was going to have a son and they would call him John. In the same chapter angel Gabriel was sent by God to Virgin Mary to announce to her that she would conceive and bear a son who would be called Jesus. Angels go before us, stay with us and follow after us. They are as near to those who do not see them as they are to those who see them. However, unlike the Holy Spirit who indwells and seals men, angels do not indwell men. Angels do not age, get sick or die.

In Hebrews 1:14 the word of God says "Are they not ministering spirits, sent forth to minister for them who shall be heirs of salvation". In Psalms 34:7 the word of God says, "The angel of the Lord encampeth round about them that fear him, and delivereth them". Angels service is limited to those saved or will be saved, but due to God's mercy they do help almost everyone. Angels serve humans and not humans serving angels. Angels are part of God's plan. We know that angels walk among us, whether you can see them or not. We are encouraged in Hebrews 13:2 "do not forget to show hospitality to strangers, for by so doing some people have shown hospitality to angels without knowing". This applies to Abraham in Genesis 18 when angelic visitors appeared to him as men. God can use angels to accomplish His assignment to His people. Angels can instruct as the angel instructed Hagar to return to her mistress Sarah and submit to her, Genesis 16:9; angels can help as seen when Daniel was thrown in the lions' den. Daniel answered the king who came to check on him in the morning "My God has sent his angel, and hath shut the lions' mouths, that they have not hurt me: forasmuch as before him innocence was found in me, and also before thee, O king, have I done no hurt": Daniel 6:22; Angels deliver messages to people as when the angel told Mary that the Holy Ghost shall come upon Mary and overshadow her and that the child born shall be called the Son of

God": Luke 1:35; Angels appear in visions as when Daniel saw the vision of an angel who explained to him that God had heard the prayers he prayed but for 21 days he was held by the kings of Persia: Daniel 10:7,13. Angels protect people as seen when God told the Israelites saying "Behold I send an angel before thee to keep thee in the way, and to bring thee into the place which I have prepared.": Exodus 23:20.

As mentioned earlier, God created angels and uses them to execute his plans. They have different names and responsibilities for example Gabriel, Michael, Chrioni. Angels are entities who carry out God's will as they receive instructions from the Holy Spirit and they are not to be worshipped or glorified (Colosians 2:18). In revelation God sent an angel to John to reveal to him things that would come to pass. He then fell down at the feet of the angel wanting to worship the angel and the angel said to him "See thou do it not: for I am thy fellow servant, and of thy brethren the prophets, and of them which keep the sayings of this book; worship God" Revelations 22:9

We are cautioned against the tricks of Satan who can masquerade as an angel of light 2 Corinthians 11:14.

Angels are spirits and are not usually seen but as mentioned earlier the Holy Spirit opens the eyes of some people and they are able to see angels. We read in scripture how God sent angels to minister to his people. Some other people have experienced divine encounters with angels. I once listened to a tape by one Evangelist who was sharing a story of how she had wanted to rent a flat and went to see the man in charge of the property. Upon viewing the flat she was given another appointment to see the him. When she entered the office she was given an envelope, which had the exact amount of money, required to pay for rent. She was told some men who looked like Arabs came in without knocking and delivered the envelope. Those were angels who delivered that money. Another sister shared that she had an accident that gave her back pain and attended Accident and Emergency but due to the long wait decided to go home. Since her car was damaged, she was worried how she was going to go for work as she used to work at night. As she lay on her bed with lights switched off, she just saw an angel who delivered a message asking her to go and see her boss and also showed her the car the boss was going to give her. When she got to work her boss gave her the exact car which the angel had told her about.

I read about a Missionary in India Mark Buntain who experienced devastating floods that threatened his work for the poor. He had to be evacuated from the area and while he was in the evacuation plane a man sat next to him who started encouraging him and advising him on how best the work of the lord can be done following these floods. When the hostess came to get orders, he gave his orders but when he looked on the seat next to him, the man had vanished. He looked everywhere in the small plane but could not see the man. He then realised that an angel had visited him.

I have been blessed to be among the few people who have experienced these divine angelic encounters. Some people might ask how did it happen that I have had these divine encounters. Could it be that I am an intercessor who has a hunger for God and prayer, or may be because I fast, I can only say that I do not know since I know there are people who pray and fast more than I do, therefore I fall short of all these areas.

From the time I was born again, God would open my eyes and see that if I was driving, I could actually see angels with me in front of the car, at the back and on each side. If I was on a plane I would see the same. More than twenty years ago we were travelling from Zambia to a Pan African Women Conference in Malawi. We were supposed to communicate with our hosts in Malawi but the phones would not get through. All of a sudden God opened my eyes and I saw the angel busy fixing the line and the phone was restored.

Sometimes I would not see the angels at work but would actually see their work after releasing them to intervene in situations. While I was training at City University London for my Registered Nursing career as a mature student, I had just sat for my 2nd year exams and went to Zambia for a holiday. I then had a dream that I had failed my exam. I told my late husband the dream and told him to pray with me to release angels to add more marks to enable me pass the examinations. We prayed and believed that what we prayed for had been done. When I came back to London, the results for the examinations were out on the Notice Board and I went and checked that I had passed. Then I proceeded to go and get my feedback of the examination. I was surprised to see that initially I had failed the examination by a few marks, when the External Examiner remarked the examination, he cancelled the marks given to me by the internal examiner and gave me more marks, which enabled me, pass the examination.

One day as a Registered Nurse I was scheduled to do home visits and give house bound patients their annual flu vaccinations. It was a very cold winter day and after seeing few patients, I needed to proceed to another patient and although I had a map with me, I couldn't locate the house. I suddenly saw an angel in front of me clothed in white and I started following the angel who went ahead of me. The angel stopped at a junction and waited and as I approached the junction the angel disappeared. When I arrived at the junction and looked ahead, that was the road I was looking for.

Another day I had a dream, in which a man was behind me in a room, but his feet were suspended and I was telling a colleague to say someone opened the door and just went but then another man was behind me with his face had like stars glittering. My colleague said she couldn't see the person. Then wondering why my colleague couldn't see the person, I turned to him and said "are you an angel", then he replied and said "I am a messenger, I have brought you a message". He said these words three times and he came down and went out of the door. Two days later, a sister in the Lord who is an evangelist called me early in the morning and said "I can't wait to tell you this dream I had". Then she went ahead and told me that she had a dream and in that dream an angel appeared to me and brought me a gift, which all admired and were praising God for the gift.

I had been suffering from terrible abdominal pains and doctors suspected it could be serious therefore referred me urgently to have a scan. An appointment had been made done for the scan but before that date attended 7 days of intense prayers by by my pastor, Pastor Matthew Ashimolowo. I came straight from work and the church was packed. I suddenly saw a very huge angel who had a sealable bag. He started packing stones into this bag and sealed it and took it away. When I went for a scan after a few days, there was no evidence of what they were suspecting. All the pains had gone and I was healed by God's grace.

Another night I had been worshiping the Lord and slept around 01.00am. I then went for work in Central London. I was on the train, which was fully packed. I then just closed my eyes and God opened my eyes to see a very huge angel. The Holy Spirit then spoke and told me and said just wanted to assure me of His presence. After work I had planned to have an early night since I had slept late the previous night but as I was going home my mobile phone rang and when I answered a daughter in the Lord was telling me that she had a friend who travelled from outside London who wanted to come over to my place for prayer.

I told her that since I was just coming from work, I would like to have a bath and then call her. I called and asked whether we should pray on the phone but she said they would just come over. Even though I was tired, I asked the Holy Spirit to reveal to me and guide me to pray right as they came. When they came in, her friend said there was such Godly presence inside the flat as they entered. We then started praying and the Holy Spirit gave me a vision which confirmed what the friend saw in a vision earlier. She then said that she was going to say something which she had seen while we were praying. She continued to say that what she had seen, she had never seen in her life before. She then went on to say that as we were praying, she saw an angel next to me. She also said that angels were going to appear to me much more. I also told them about the angelic encounter earlier in the day.

Soon after that I slept just like any ordinary night and had a dream. In this dream an angel came and sat at the edge of my bed and asked me to write down the names of God. I had a book in which I wrote the names of God such as Jehovah Jireh, Jehovah Shalom, Jehovah Nissi and once I finished writing the angel of God told me that there was one more name I didn't write and I said "Jehovah Sabaoth" to which the angels agreed. I was advised that whenever we call on God, we must call Him by the name, which applies, to our need. For example if we need healing, we call him by Jehovah Rapha, if it is peace; we call on Jehovah, our peace.

One day I attended a conference and in that conference one of the men of God preaching said there are a lot of angels in that place. Someone tapped me on the shoulder and handed me a note, which asked me to confirm my name. I looked back to ask who had given me that note and I was pointed to a man who didn't say anything but was just smiling. I wondered who that person was and when I turned to let him know we can talk later after the conference, he was gone.

When I was so overwhelmed by these angelic visitations and encounters I sought to seek counsel from the man of God Dr Mike Murdock, being a protégé' and partner of his ministry. When I explained to him the supernatural experiences I was encountering he explained to me that angels usually brought messages and advised me not to share these experiences anyhow. He further told me that I was blessed to have these encounters as he joked that he had told God that if he was allowed to experience angelic visitations, he would double his tithe. He further advised me to buy some books by Billy Graham and Roland

Buck, who himself had experienced much deeper encounters in order to understand more about angels.

BENEFITS OF THE MINISTRY OF ANGELS

Angels carry the word of God to perform it when you confess who God is to you and what He will do to you. Shadrack Mishek and Abednego confessed that God would deliver them and God sent an angel to prevent them from burning.

Jesus when tempted in the wilderness confessed the word of God and the devil finally left and angels came and ministered to Him.

Angels guide you as they guided Moses "Behold, I send an Angel before thee, to keep thee in the way, and to bring thee into the place which I have prepared in the desert" as said in Exodus 23:20 Therefore release angels of God before you go anywhere.

Angels make the word of God effective; therefore release ministering angels to make God's word effective.

Angels do God's pleasure to believers as said in Psalms 103:20 "Bless the LORD, ye his angels, that excel in strength, that do his commandments, hearkening unto the voice of his word."

Angels build a hedge of protection as indicated in Job 1:10 "Hast not thou made an hedge about him, and about his house, and about all that he hath on every side? thou hast blessed the work of his hands, and his substance is increased in the land."

Angels execute deliverance from danger as said in Psalms 34:7 " The angel of the Lord encampeth around about them that fear him and delivereth him" and 2 Kings 6:17 says " And Elisha prayed, and said, LORD, I pray thee, open his eyes, that he may see. And the LORD opened the eyes of the young man; and he saw: and, behold, the mountain was full of horses and chariots of fire round about Elisha."

Angels ensure and execute your destiny as in Exodus 23:20 mentioned above.

Angels trample over the devil and protect you Psalms 91:11-13

For he shall give his angels charge over thee, to keep thee in all thy ways.

They shall bear thee up in their hands, lest thou dash thy foot against a stone.

Thou shalt tread upon the lion and adder: the young lion and the dragon shalt thou trample under feet. Psalms 35:5-6 "Let them as chaff before the wind: and let the angel of the Lord chase them. Let their way be dark and slippery: and let the angel of the Lord persecute them."

We need to understand that when we pray, God sends his angels to bring answers but the devil fights to prevent answers from being delivered. In Daniel 10:12-13, the word of God says " Then said he unto me, Fear not, Daniel: for from the first day that thou didst set thine heart to understand, and to chasten thyself before thy God, thy words were heard, and I am come for thy words.

But the prince of the kingdom of Persia withstood me one and twenty days: but, lo, Michael, one of the chief princes, came to help me; and I remained there with the kings of Persia.

In Daniel 9:23 the word of God says " At the beginning of thy supplications the commandment came forth, and I am come to shew thee; for thou art greatly beloved: therefore understand the matter, and consider the vision" This means when we pray God sends His messengers in motion. The natural realm they have speed does not limit them.

Angels are busy. Jacob on his way from Beersheba to Haran set down to sleep when the sun had set, he therefore took stones and made pillows and Genesis 28:2 says "And he dreamed, and behold a ladder set up on the earth, and the top of it reached to heaven: and behold the angels of God ascending and descending on it."

TRIUMPHING OVER CHALLENGES AND TRIALS

In John 16:33 Jesus Christ said "These things I have spoken unto you, that in me ye might have peace. In the world ye shall have tribulation: but be of good cheer, I have overcome the world".

Any person faces problems in life and they come in different shapes. Jesus did not want us to be ignorant of the fact that we may face challenges as Christians. It may be financial, or wayward child, or marital challenges, family or work related or spiritual warfare but they all come to humans and it does not matter how spiritual one may be or may not be. It does not mean that God has forsaken you. His word in Isaiah 41:10 says fear thou not; for I am with thee: be not dismayed; for I am thy God: I will strengthen thee; yea, I will help thee; yea, I will uphold thee with the right hand of my righteousness. Hebrews 13:5b says for he hath said, I will never leave thee, nor forsake thee.

God assures us in Isaiah 43:2 which says when thou passes through the waters, I will be with thee; and through the rivers, they shall not overflow thee: when thou walkest through the fire, thou shalt not be burned; neither shall the flame kindle upon thee.

1 Corinthians 10:13 says There hath no temptation taken hold of you but such as is common to man. But God is faithful; He will not suffer you to be tempted beyond that which ye are able to bear, but with the temptation will also make a way to escape, that ye may be able to bear it.

Sometimes God would tell you to do something and then the problem becomes worse and you wonder whether God was in the situation. In Luke 8:22-26 we see that Jesus told his disciples to go over to the other side and in the process they encountered a storm that threatened their very lives. How could they encounter these problems when it was Jesus who had told them to go over the other side. This will tell us that even if you are with Jesus, you will still experience problems but just remember that Jesus overcame at the cross and when you are with Jesus victory is assured. When you face challenges the time looks so long but we have assurance from the word of God in Psalms 30:5 that weeping may endure for a night but joy cometh in the morning which means no matter what you are going through it has an expiry date and your joy will return.

In 1 Samuel 30:6 we read that after David came back from battle having won victories against his enemies, he came home to find that the Amelikites had destroyed his home and his family had been taken captive. The bible records that he and his men fell down and wept until they could weep no more. But David knew that weeping would not yield anything. He didn't continue to stay down but decided to ask God what he would do next whether to pursue the troop and overtake them to which the Lord gave him a go ahead and said "pursue, for you shall surely overtake and without fail recover all" David encouraged himself and sought the Lord's guidance.

Let the problem that comes your way make you kneel down more and pray and get closer to God. Problems do come and you can chose to make the problem be a stumbling block or a bridge to your next level. To have self-pity doesn't help but rather seek for a solution out of the problem. I watched a video of a young man in Africa who experienced famine in his village, which led him to study science books, which helped him, develop a device that would bring him a solution and make him known in the world. He didn't sit and complain but rather he was willing to do something about his situation. Most men of God who say that the biggest battles bring the biggest victories have encouraged me. Learn to encourage yourself in the Lord knowing that this too shall pass. Romans 8:28 says "and we know that all things work together for good to them that love God, to them who are the called according to *his* purpose. Sometimes God takes us to the bottom in order to get us to the top. Once you reach the bottom, there is no other place to go apart from getting up. Joseph went through so many problems among others, being sold by his own brothers before reaching a position of prominence. When Potiphar's wife falsely accused him of attempted rape, he was imprisoned and it was in prison that he met the butler who introduced him to Pharaoh and he later became Pharaoh's second in command. In Genesis 50:20 he told his brothers. "God turned into good what you meant for evil." He is still in the business of doing that even today. He will turn your pain into gain and your scars into stars. God knows exactly what lessons you need to learn along the path of life before you get to your next level. When hard times come, and when trials fall upon us they are not meant to defeat us but to be the means to a greater spiritual victory. They are not intended to make us weaker but to make us stronger. Trials are not permanent torments but are temporary tests that reveal our trust in Christ.

In order for you to overcome the storms of life, you have to know that God is with you and that he will never leave you nor forsake you. Not a sparrow falls to the ground without His notice. You have to know where to turn to and focus on the Lord. God rewards those who earnestly seek him. Psalms 34:19 says Many are the afflictions of the righteous: but the LORD delivereth him out of them all.

Many times when trials come your way you may ask yourself why you would have to go through what you are going through. The solution is to surrender and trust God even when there are no answers. Deutronomy 29:29 says "the secret things belong unto the LORD our God: but those things which are revealed belong unto us and to our children for ever, that we may do all the words of this law." Therefore we may not know the answers but God knows. The late man of God Andre Crouch sang a song which says that without passing through problems, you wouldn't know that God can solve them and he said through it all, he learnt to trust in Jesus and depend upon His word. Proverbs 24:10 says "if you faint in the day of adversity your strength is small". Great men and women do not quit. They are overcomers. They ignore difficulties, resist tiredness, frustration and defeat and do not give up. Only the weak fail or quit when the going gets tough. There is an old saying which says "when the going gets tough the tough gets going.

We can also learn some lessons from the eagle. The eagle uses the storm's wind to lift it higher and once it finds the wind of the storm, it uses the raging storm to lift him above the clouds. This action gives the eagle an opportunity to glide and rest its wings. That is why the eagle loves the storm. Like the eagle we can use the storms of life to rise to greater heights. In order to overcome and be an achiever you need to relish challenges and use them as a bridge to your next level. 1 Thessalonians 5:18 says " In every thing give thanks: for this is the will of God in Christ Jesus concerning you."

In conclusion when you encounter a problem:

- Acknowledge that you have a problem, do not be in denial
- Stop avoiding the problem but embrace the pain because you cannot go over the problem or under it, neither can you go round it but you can only go through it. If you embrace the pain, you will be able to conquer the problem
- Stop feeling sorry for yourself don't throw a pity party it will not help
- Do not be tempted to compare what other people have been through as this only makes you resentful, bitter, jealous and unproductive and besides you do not know what other people have been through too.
- Remember that God has allowed that problem knowing that you are fully equipped for the battle
- Seek God for a solution, rejoice and praise God in that situation
- Pray Until Something Happens (PUSH)

PURSUING YOUR VISION

Finally let me say that as one advances in age, there is the apathy that most people believe that there is nothing more left to do in life and most people believe that. However, we should get encouragement and learn from people that have achieved greater things in their later age in life and be motivated ourselves to do exploits. One may have had dreams when they were young to desire to achieve certain things in life such as writing their first book, starting a new career, release an album, go back to university, have children, marry their dream woman or man or even be a model or an actor or actress or be a film producer but as years went by they begin to lose interest in accomplishing their dreams because of their advancing in age.

Age should not be a deterring factor to accomplishing one's dream. Every dream that one has can be accomplished with determination. When you are determined, you are fearless, bold and brave. You will not go with the flow of the majority. You will be able to see your God given vision clearly and achieve it despite opposition from people whose faith may not be at your level who may want to stop you by discouraging you. Many times when you share a 20 meter vision to someone who can only see a 5 meter vision, their first words would be that you cannot achieve that and they would give you examples of how other people had failed. I remember when I first came to UK I met my former workmate I worked with at the Bank of Zambia. When I told her that I was planning to bring my children over to join me, she started explaining how difficult it was to bring your family here in UK. I already had my two children with me at that time. I went ahead and brought the other two except my 2nd born who couldn't come as she was married. When I was still in Zambia working for the Central Bank, I shared with a man of God about my plans to have my two youngest children get into a private school, which was run by the Mines and was quite expensive. He looked at me and said, "you have a lot of faith" to which I agreed that God was going to do it. It was very difficult to get into that school as places were limited since they took children from people who had good jobs in the mines. The background was that I had applied for a place for my daughter at a government school but due to her age she was not given a place. I had refused to lie about her age whereas a colleague's child was accepted because she added one more year to her original years. I then went to God in prayer and said "Lord I was faithful to you by refusing to lie about my daughter's age, I ask that you be faithful to me and grant me a place for my daughter at this beautiful school." The Lord was surely faithful as my daughter was accepted to God's glory. However, my late husband Lawrence and I had gone to see the headmistress seven times because we were determined despite what other people's opinions. When it came to my youngest son's turn to get into that school, we went several times to see the headmistress again. One day my late husband determined, took the money into his briefcase and went to see the headmistress and told her he had come to pay for the school fees. My son was accepted and he started school at the private school

Determination requires that you walk by faith and have a winning attitude to life. When you are determined you never quit. When you are determined you have made up your mind that despite failure or discouragement you can dream again and succeed. Immanuel Kant, the German philosopher who was born in

1724 wrote his best philosophical works at the age of 74. At 80 Lord Alfred Tennyson the poet who was born in 1809 wrote, "Crossing the bar" and Titian the artist who was born in 1488 painted his famous "Allegory of the Battle of Lepanto" at the age of 98. There have been many outstanding achievers like Verdi who penned his classic "Ave Maria" at the age of eighty-five. At ninety, Justice Oliver Wendell Holmes who was born in 1841 set down some of his most brilliant opinions. One of the most powerful men in the world was President Ronald Reagan who was born in 1911 and became the 40th American President at the age of 70. When we go to the word of God we find out that Noah was over six hundred years when he came out of the ark after the flood and helped to start the world all over again. Moses was 80 years old when he led the children of Israel to freedom from slavery. Caleb was 40 years when he was sent by Moses to spy the land of Canaan. At 85 years old he said "as yet I am as strong this day as I was in the day that Moses sent me, as my strength was then, even so, is my strength now for war, both to go out and to come in. Now therefore give me this mountain whereof the Lord spoke in that day." Joshua 14:11-12.

Psalms 92:14 the psalmist David wrote "They shall still bear fruit in old age", which means that we should continue bearing fruits even in old age. In Psalms 103:1,5 David says "Bless the Lord O my soul: and all that is within me, bless his holy name. Who satisfies thy mouth with good things: so that thy youth is renewed like the eagle's." An eagle goes through a very difficult situation to bring about its transformation just as one would have to go through some challenging situations to bring about change in one's life. Phillipians 4:13 says "I can do all things through Christ Jesus who strengthens me. It doesn't give us a limitation of age.

We should continue to have the enthusiasm that we had as youths in order to achieve and accomplish greater heights to the glory of God. In an article I read in UCB, Alexander Dumas was asked how does he grow gracefully and his reply was "I give my time to it. "It was also mentioned that if you are over 50, let your age be measured by your spiritual progress instead of a date on the calendar. Growing older does not only mean you retire, but rather re-focus. Getting order means we must discipline ourselves to continue expanding, broadening and keeping our minds active and open. In Luke 2:36-38 the word of God talks about Prophetess Anna, an eighty four year old widow who was still serving the Lord by fasting and praying night and day and never departed from the temple. Despite her age, she was still committed to serving in the house of God.

Before God delivered me I had made a vow to God that if He healed me and delivered me I would serve Him for the rest of my life. I have been born again for almost 30 years now and have come to know and believe that God is faithful and he never fails us. By God's grace I will continue to serve the Lord and do what He has called me to do for the rest of my life.

With this in mind, I am determined by the grace of God to achieve all what God has planned for my life and would like to encourage both the young and the old to pursue their dreams until they achieve. In Habakkuk 3:2 God told Habakkuk to write the vision and said "For the vision is yet for the appointed time, but at the end it shall speak, and not lie: though it tarry, wait for it ; because it will surely come, it will not tarry." Therefore even if a dream seems to take long, if you don't lose focus, it shall come to pass by God's grace.

MAKE A DECISION FOR JESUS

I am ending this book with the invitation for you to make a decision to accept Jesus as your Personal Saviour if you have not done so before. The word of God says in Romans 10:9 "That if you shall confess with thy mouth the Lord Jesus, and shall believe in thine heart that God hath raised him from the dead, thou shall be saved". I would like you to pray this prayer from your heart.

Dear Jesus, I confess that I am a sinner and I need your love and forgiveness. I repent of my sins. Come into my heart. I receive you as my Lord and Saviour. Remove my name from the book of death and write my name in the book of life and I receive your eternal life Amen."

If you have prayed this prayer you are born again and are a new creature, old things have passed away. (2 Corinthians 5:17).

www.ingramcontent.com/pod-product-compliance
Lightning Source LLC
Chambersburg PA
CBHW032036090426
42741CB00006B/840